Foodstuff

Living in an age of feast and famine

Foodstuff

Demos Collection / issue 18

Editors
John Holden
Lydia Howland
Daniel Stedman Jones

Production editor
Eddie Gibb

Cover design by The Set Up, London
Typeset by Politico's Design, London
Printed by Biddles Ltd, Guildford

Demos Collection is
published twice a year by
Demos
Elizabeth House
39 York Road
London
SE1 7NQ

tel: 020 7401 5330
fax: 020 7401 5331

mail@demos.co.uk
www.demos.co.uk

ISBN 1 84180 103 8

Demos gratefully acknowledges funding
from the Tedworth Charitable Trust for
this piece of work.

Demos is a greenhouse for new ideas
which can improve the quality of our
lives. As an independent think tank, we
aim to create an open resource of
knowledge and learning that operates
beyond traditional party politics.

We connect researchers, thinkers
and practitioners to an international
network of **people changing politics**. C
ideas regularly influence government
policy, but we also work with compan:
NGOs, colleges and professional bodie

Demos knowledge is organised around
five themes, which combine to create ne
perspectives. The themes are democracy
learning, enterprise, quality of life and
global change.

But we also understand that thinking
itself is not enough. Demos has helped
to initiate a number of practical projec
which are delivering real social benefit
through the redesign of public services

For Demos, the process is as important
as the final product. We bring togethe
people from a wide range of backgrounds to cross-fertilise ideas and
experience. By working with Demos, o
partners help us to develop sharper
insight into the way ideas shape socie

Contents

Foodstuff: Living in an age of feast and famine

4   Acknowledgements

5   Introduction: **Closing the loop** John Holden, Lydia Howland and Daniel Stedman Jones

Part 1. Understanding food culture

19 **Too rich, too thin?** Felipe Fernández-Armesto

25 **Slow down: The return to local food** Carlo Petrini

31 **Food is not fuel** Geraldine Bedell

37 **The spice of life?** David Lammy

45 **Social service** Terence Conran

51 **On the menu: why more choice isn't better** Rebecca L Spang

Part 2. Food politics, risk and trust

59 **Hot potatoes: politicians, food and risk** John Gummer

67 **Farming today: food science and subsidy** Chris Haskins

73 **Gut reaction: the real risks of food poisoning** Hugh Pennington

79 **Cultivating trust** Renate Künast

83 **'Big Food': politics and nutrition in the United States** Marion Nestle

Part 3. Well-being and social outcomes

93 **Barbecue of the vanities: nutritional advice since the Renaissance** Steven Shapin

99 **Working on the food chain gang** Jeanette Longfield

105 **Getting better: food in the NHS** Loyd Grossman

111 **Recipe for peace: the role of nutrition in social behaviour** Bernard Gesch

117 **Urban agriculture in Australia: local food, global communities** John Brisbin

123 **People – the missing ingredient** Daniel Miller

Part 4. Global hunger

131 **The rich diet, and the poor go hungry** Clare Short

139 **The politics of the empty belly** Alex de Waal

145 **Feast and famine** James Erlichman

151 **'To them that hath...': how world trade policies undermine poor producers** Barbara Stocking

million suffer from malnutrition globally. Millions of people die from over-consumption and starvation every day; US consumers spend US$29 billion on confectionery while the UN struggles to find its $1.5 billion budget. Media focus on people's misery across the world has not yet produced a successful collective endeavour for eradicating hunger. Western governments, fully committed to international development, preserve trade regimes that over-protect their own food industries while severely limiting the participation of developing countries in the new riches of the food trade.

This collection provides a panoramic view of the shifting patterns of production, consumption and culture that shape our relationships with food, and reveals a surprising range of ways in which eating affects our broader quality of life. Its dominant message is that we are spoiling the riches of contemporary food culture by adopting patterns of behaviour that are collectively dysfunctional. However, the authors also identify many different opportunities to make our treatment of food more sustainable, more just and simply more enjoyable.

First, the good news

As several of our contributors point out, many aspects of food have improved since the end of the Second World War. The level and range of affordable nutrition, and the global cuisine that we now access through television, supermarkets and high street restaurants, reflect significant progress. As Chris Haskins argues, advances in agricultural technology and management have brought more plentiful, cheaper and more hygienic food to the mass of the population.

As British society has grown more affluent, food culture has taken on an increasingly 'postmaterialist' complexion, serving needs well beyond simple survival. It is still less than 50 years since rationing ended in the UK but, within that time, supermarkets have become secular cathedrals, offering to meet all our lifestyle needs, expanding into banking, dating, childcare and learning provision, and developing around them a host of hangers-on, cultish visionaries and oppositional forces. As a result, they have acquired an almost mythical significance in the public imagination.

Hours of daytime and evening TV programming are devoted to food and its preparation, with celebrity chefs high in the public consciousness. We also see successful attempts to take a different path: farmers markets have proliferated over the last five years, and the organic movement, once scorned by supermarkets and the National Farmers Union alike, is now a significant part of the mainstream. The diversity on offer, both within and outside the supermarket, reflects a growing collective confidence in our food culture.

An unpleasant aftertaste

But these advances mask persistent and troubling problems, and also appear to contribute to new risks, costs and hardships. In 2002, as a Demos study showed, food poverty remains a significant, if little noticed, problem in the UK.[1] Many low-income households still struggle, and often fail, to attain a nutritious diet. This is a much more complex problem than simply being able to afford cheap food – other factors such as transport, storage and the pressure exerted by children over their parents all play a part. On average, the relative spend on food in the household budget has fallen significantly. Paradoxically, in a society increasingly characterised by 'mass affluence' and cheap, abundant food, poor diet is a persistent problem.

This is not the only difficulty. The growth of modern food psychoses, including chronic obesity, anorexia and bulimia, is widely lamented but has failed to elicit effective, shared responses. Global media and celebrity culture have produced a set of profoundly damaging psychosocial pressures. Body image has become a painfully important source of identity and self-esteem, yet our popular culture still promotes systematically distorted images of what healthy, attractive bodies (both male and female) should look like.

Throughout Western society, food is aggressively marketed as 'sexy' while advertisers and the media simultaneously promote the belief that sexy means thin. Thinness as a signifier of affluence and desirability is a recent development, as Felipe Fernández-Armesto shows. Historically, conspicuous consumption was a sign of high status; now, the rich would rather

1 Hitchman C, Christie I, Harrison M and Lang T, 2002, *Inconvenience Food*, Demos, London.

starve than join the swelling masses of the overweight. If this trend persists in tandem with that of obesity, many more young people will be dissatisfied with their bodies, with increasingly serious results.

Alongside these deep concerns, we are busy manufacturing a whole new set of food fears arising from our ability to engineer abundance: vCJD, foot-and-mouth disease, confusion over GM and escalating concern at the political influence of corporate food interests all define the new food landscape. One new concern caused by our proliferating food waste is a rat population greater than that of humans in the UK, fed to the point of plague.

While most of us are able to enjoy unprecedented choice and diversity, we are also beset by guilt, fear and confusion, bombarded with new information about what and how to eat, unsure what to feed our children and anxious that we might already have made choices that will lead to disaster. Although we indulge, enjoy and agonise in the West, the world is still blighted by hunger.

The contours of food culture

Visible food culture is dominated by principles of choice, convenience, affordability and disposability. The growth of supermarkets, fast food and take away are a response to consumer demand. While shaping our lives, food also has to fit in with the conditions of modern living. Work–life imbalance drives the cash-rich and time-poor towards convenience foods, processed snacks and food on the run. But these pressures often run counter to the essence of improving people's lives; speed, cheapness and excess are likely to be the enemies of quality, conviviality and well-being.

As Rebecca Spang illustrates, using the menu as an example, the rise of individualism has given us an unrealistic understanding of the meaning of choice. Our decision-making mechanisms obscure the real consequences and connections between our consumption options and the systems of production and distribution that underpin them. We often choose in a vacuum, in ways that ignore the collective and interactive impact of our actions.

Our attitudes to food are influenced by more than just the rational demands of economics, convenience and the instant sating of appetite. We are hardwired by genes and programmed by our culture to behave in particular ways. Only very recently in human history have we achieved an oversupply of food and, as James Erlichman points out, we remain genetically predisposed to storing food and conserving energy – a biological leftover from the hunter gatherer period of evolutionary history.

John Gummer suggests that we have maintained a mystical relationship with food and its purity. This attitude, formed deep in our history, explains not just our contradictory reactions to science and technology, but the curiously symbolic place that food occupies in politics and the instinctive reactions that food crises generate. Even as a modern, industrialised nation we still crave a spiritual connection with the land – part of the reason we continue to subsidise agricultural production so heavily. The idea of losing national self-sufficiency in food production is deeply troubling, even though food is an area which, like most of our other economic activities, has become increasingly interconnected with other parts of the world.

Equally significant, if perhaps more mundane, is the role that habituation plays in forming and sustaining our patterns of food behaviour, and our addiction to unhealthy or unsustainable forms of consumption. The food industry has become a powerful force in defining what we eat, and the food policy arena in developed countries, particularly the US, is dominated by vested interests. Marion Nestle (a nutrition expert) examines the umbilical relationship between food and politics in the US, and describes the connections that undermine the development of a responsible and healthy food culture. Consistency of advice about nutrition and diet has evaded us for centuries, as Steven Shapin points out, and neither the cacophony of expertise nor the incoherence of responses is new.

Webs and chains: reconnecting food systems

How can we begin to make sense of our predicament? One starting point is to recognise that food outcomes are linked through a number of complex systems; finding ways to fill the vacuum between industrialisation and consumerism may provide some routes to progress. Holism and sustainability are strong themes in several essays: John Brisbin, Carlo Petrini and Daniel Miller emphasise the significance of the growing detachment of the consumer from the production process. The dehumanisation of food chains can be countered by the development of what Brisbin refers to as strong local food networks that promote local produce, create and help to sustain local knowledge, and reinforce good eating habits. Petrini demonstrates how sustainability, conviviality and biotic health can flow from choosing to eat high-quality, locally produced food.

However, localism and shortening supply chains are unlikely to provide complete answers: we also need to address our position within the global food system. Solutions to food poverty and inequality will only be found when food education is embraced and taught within local communities. Miller envisages a world where education, facilitated by emerging technologies, enables a much richer understanding of the human dimension to the food chain, allowing a partial reintegration of production and consumption through collective awareness of the impacts of purchasing decisions.

The systems that govern and contextualise food – global trade agreements, transport and communications infrastructures, weather patterns, cultural preferences and taboos – are individually complex. However, in tackling global hunger, a sustainable strategy has to integrate them, as Clare Short, Alex de Waal and Barbara Stocking all make clear in different ways. Development aid has to engage with the economic, social and epidemiological factors that systematically undermine the ability of African governments, in particular, to ensure that all their people are properly fed. The old paradigm, where both the need for food aid and food aid itself resulted from the surpluses generated by the protectionist policies of developed countries, needs to be overturned. Coherent and unified policies are required to create an equitable trade in food.

Another major concern arises from the effect of modern farming practices, eg monocultures, on the natural environment. Disease spreads most quickly where uniformity is found, and this is why genetic diversity is so important.

Food and social outcomes

Many contributions in this collection focus on the connections between eating and social outcomes. Food is a classic example of silo-based policy-making, artificially separated into different areas of governance. Government has traditionally thought in terms of production (subsidies, international relations, rural policy), manufacture and retail (food safety, planning, transport) and consumption (advice, but not too much of it, lest the producers, retailers and media object).

Several authors urge a more enlightened and evidence-based approach to the use of nutrition in social and institutional settings. As Jeanette Longfield argues, if sustainable development and consumption are such cornerstones of government policy, why does public sector catering have such a bad record?

Loyd Grossman makes a convincing case that high-quality medical and primary care are most effective when complemented by good food and a balanced diet. Developing effective public health policies might be easier if the NHS provided hospital patients with a nutritional diet, as the new food programme aims to do. Bernard Gesch cites evidence that changes to the diet of prisoners may have significant, beneficial effects on their behaviour. In the same vein, a number of schools are converting to additive-free school dinners to help promote concentration and learning. A clear extension of this programme would be to replace soft drinks machines with adequate supplies of drinking water in schools; an initiative that should be made mandatory nationwide.

If institutions can do more to support positive social outcomes through their food practices, then the personal mores of eating together, in and out, are even more influential. Terence Conran attributes the phenomenal success of café culture and restaurants to people's desire for conviviality and the growth of disposable income, while Geraldine Bedell argues powerfully that we should rediscover the ways in which food can serve our quality of life and social relationships. David Lammy suggests that the diversity of food cultures and collective cuisines found in his Tottenham constituency should be understood as a contribution to social capital and community capacity. Eating is not only a factor in public health, but potentially a route to social inclusion.

Risk and imperfect science

Public debate may have matured slightly since the days of Edwina Currie and BSE, but there is still deep unease about the extent to which government should and could protect us from the dangers created by modern food systems. Our infantile collective attitude to food leads us to seek security even as we push our manipulation of nature to new extremes. The result is a public that seeks absolute guarantees of food safety and, when science can't provide them, passes the buck on to ministers, forcing them to assume responsibility for things beyond their control.

Paranoia is amplified by a media that pounces upon food crises with gusto, making it harder for the public to understand the concept of risk, let alone make a rational assessment of it. Hugh Pennington suggests that politicians must take their fair share of responsibility for hiding behind what he calls the imperfect application of science. As Gummer points out, ministers have felt it essential to foster an illusion of certainty while being fully aware that science is a process of empirical accumulation with conclusions that are always liable to change.

We must negotiate a new approach, underpinned by a more honest, searching discourse between experts, ministers, the wider 'body politic' and the public, in which all actors have a responsible role, and with transparent accountability structures. Set up in 2000 as a useful first step in this approach, the Food Standards Agency has been relatively successful in creating a more open culture of information and debate, and has the virtue of putting some food issues at arm's length from government. However, its remit and powers are limited and no matter how well it functions, it cannot keep food away from politics altogether.

Rather than spinning a predetermined position, ministers should be lead a continuing debate and admit that limited scientific knowledge is not always the best starting point for a grown-up discussion. Parliament, government agencies and quangos must attempt to address public concerns through better provision of information and more rigorous regulation, and the media must take a more responsible role in communicating with the public. A concerted and collective attempt must be made to raise awareness that risk is usually relative and seldom absolute; providing sufficient information will help people to offset one set of risks against another. The disparity between our individual food choices and their cumulative impact on society as a whole could thus be lessened by solving the contradictions in our attitudes to knowledge, safety and risk.

The politics of good food

The first principle of food policy should be that adequate food intake is the most basic right of every citizen. No one should go hungry in a nation as rich as ours, and the provision of basic nutrition must be a cornerstone of any civilised society. The priority of food policy must be similar to that of energy policy: 'security and diversity of supply'. Ultimately responsible for basic food safety, trade relations and the long-term stewardship of the land, governments must create the conditions for one generation to pass healthy and productive resources to the next.

At an international level, food policy should serve the interests of global justice and the eradication of hunger. The most obvious candidates are reform of the EU Common Agricultural Policy and steps towards a more open trade system for developing countries with a shared goal of more sustainable agriculture and food production explicitly built into them.

Basic and sufficient nutrition on a national and global scale are the fundamental foundations. The second building block is a move towards a better diet for all through changes in the production and consumption of food; a move away from the traditional emphasis on producer interests and towards a stronger alliance between consumers, politics and governance. Producer and consumer interests may be in conflict in specific instances but they converge at the highest level. A sustainable agricultural sector and a healthy, well-fed population are inclusive aims: food production, trade, taxation and regulation should reflect the long-term need to maintain the natural systems that underpin nutritional needs.

Enlightened consumer choice can improve standards of production and distribution. At present, the food industry gets away with labelling and information that shed little light. How can we be informed consumers when we can't tell how far vegetables have travelled, or which pesticides were sprayed on our fruit? We might wish to know, yet are never told, the daily wage of the Colombian campesino who harvested the beans for our morning cup of coffee. Food labels sometimes imitate the logic of Alice in Wonderland: bacon containing 10 per cent water can be labelled as containing none at all.

Knowledge about sourcing, processing, additives and conditions of production – whether provided at point of sale or on request – are all vital tools for consumer empowerment and true diversity of supply. Such knowledge may fuel a robust confrontation with producer interest groups and retailers, but only by changing our food culture can we reduce our already high rates of obesity, cancer and heart disease.

Government procurement should reflect a far greater interest in food issues and lead by example, as Longfield suggests. Catering in hospitals, schools, prisons and civil service canteens should be connected to an agenda of sustainable food production and societal health promotion. Public inspection bodies, such as OFSTED, should take food into account in their reporting regimes in order to bring the worst performing up to the level of the best. Government departments should take more active responsibility for the diet of people in their care rather than simply setting standards for nutritional intake. They should back research into the behavioural effects of food consumption by changing the systems of the institutions they control.

In particular, the government should look again at the way in which budgets and finances discourage high-quality food in schools. Nutritional standards for school meals were reintroduced in 2000, but schools are encouraged to meet those standards at minimal cost – often as low as 40p per meal – with no regard for quality.

The creation of nutrition strategies and the appointment of nutrition tsars in the devolved administrations is an encouraging start on the journey towards a better diet. However, despite rumours that they are imminent, neither is yet in place in England; in any case, the tsar approach is only a way of kickstarting the process.

Equally important is the consumption of fatty, salty and sugared processed foods that are always heavily advertised; these foods have direct societal costs. People's freedom to consume them should not be directly restricted, but a system of taxation should be introduced to redress their effects, in the same way as cigarettes and alcohol. The proceeds of such taxation could then be used to support healthier and more beneficial forms of consumption, particularly at a local community level.

The third priority of food policy should be a positive agenda of well-being, so that we can all enjoy high-quality food. Social change must be founded on the principle of well-informed citizens with genuine choice. From the earliest age, food for health and enjoyment should be a central principle of education and part of the national curriculum, with mealtimes as a component of citizenship and social education.

Government must encourage the trend towards a return to the local. Initiatives such as farmers markets, box schemes, community farms and good old-fashioned allotments, provide better, fresher produce, reduce 'food miles' and help create a more sustainable agriculture. They forge links between producers and consumers and educate people in the realities of food sources, helping to bridge the artificial gap between town and country.

Governments do not and should not control our food habits, but they can help to shape them for our mutual benefit by taking a clear lead in two specific areas of the debate. First, they must create a platform for, and then instigate, a mature discussion about risk, responsibility and accountability that promotes honest dialogue between the expert and the lay person. Second, they must lead by example by ensuring that public sector catering promotes sustainability and well-being.

The policies of government will always be driven as much by our collective food behaviour as by matters of principle. If we can learn to prioritise our well-being rather than just our instant craving, we will be on the way to a politics that can achieve far more for us, both as individuals and as a society. Given its essential nature and its pervasive influence, food is as good a place to start as any.

Part 1

Understanding Food Culture

Too rich, too thin?

Fat was once fashionable, but overabundance means people are dying to be slim

Felipe Fernández-Armesto

Food was the basis of the first class system. Superior nourishment is the most primitive form of privilege. Socially differentiating cuisines, however, occurred relatively late and, until recently, were found only in some parts of the world. Originally, quantity mattered more than quality.

The gigantic appetite has normally commanded prestige in almost every society, partly as a sign of prowess and partly, perhaps, as an indulgence accessible only to wealth. Gluttony may be a sin but it has never been classed as a crime. On the contrary, it can be socially functional. Big appetites stimulate production and generate surplus – leftovers on which lesser eaters can feed. So long as the food supply is unthreatened, eating a lot is an act of heroism and justice, similar in effect to other such acts, such as fighting off enemies and propitiating the gods. It is usual to find the same sort of people engaged in all three tasks. Legendary feats of digestion were chronicled in antiquity, like heroes' tallies of battle victims, wanderers' odysseys or tyrants' laws. Every day, Maximinus the Thracian drank an amphora of wine and ate 40 or 50 pounds of meat. Clodius Albinus was celebrated because he could eat 500 figs, a basket of peaches, 10 melons, 20 pounds of grapes, 100 garden warblers and 400 oysters at a sitting. Guido of Spoleto was refused the French throne because he was a frugal eater. Charlemagne could not manage dietary temperance and refused his physicians' advice to mitigate his digestive problems by eating boiled instead of roasted food: this was the gustatory equivalent of Roland's refusal to summon reinforcements in battle – recklessness hallowed by risk. To comply would have been an act of self-derogation.[1]

Such triumphs of heroic eating were not considered selfish. The rich man's table is part of the machinery of wealth distribution. His demand attracts supply. His waste feeds the poor. Food sharing is a fundamental form of gift exchange, cement of societies; chains of food distribution are social shackles. They create relationships of dependence, suppress revolutions and keep client classes in their place. The story is told of how Consuelo Vanderbilt, when she became châtelaine of Blenheim Palace, reformed the method by which leftovers were distributed among the poor neighbours of the estate: the broken meats were still slopped into jerry cans and wheeled out to the beneficiaries, but Consuelo was fastidious enough to insist that, for the first time in the history of the house, the courses be separated – meat from fish, sweets from savouries, and so on. Consuelo's generosity belongs to a long tradition of noblesse oblige, scattered with crumbs from the rich man's table, haunted by the ghosts of guests from the highways and byways.[2]

The redistribution of health

The tradition goes back at least to the redistributive palace storehouses of early agrarian civilisations. The labyrinth of Knossos contained no minotaurs but it was filled with oil jars and bins of grain. Ancient Egypt was a food engine and the pharaonic economy was dedicated to a cult of the abundance of the everyday: not individual abundance, for most people lived on bread and beer in amounts only modestly above subsistence level, but a surplus garnered and guarded against hard times, at the disposal of the state and the priests. The temple built to commemorate Ramses II had storehouses big enough to feed 20,000 people for a year. The taxation yields proudly painted on the walls of a vizier's tomb are an illustrated menu for hoarders on a monumental scale: sacks of barley, piles of loaves,

1 Montanari M, 1994, *The culture of food*, Blackwell, Oxford, pp 10–11, pp 22–6.
2 Girouard M, 1978, *Life in the English country house*, Yale University Press, New Haven CT, p 12.

hundreds of head of livestock.[3] Ancient Egypt was unusual in having, like the contemporary West, an aesthetic of thinness. Gods and rulers were lissom, columnar. There, like here, you could never be too rich or too thin. In most cultures, the master of abundance is fat – that is how he commands confidence among people who depend on him for food. Greatness goes with greatness of girth.

Reverence for excess remains widespread in the world outside the west. Modern Trobriand Islanders relish the prospect of a feast so big that 'we shall eat until we vomit.' A South African saying is, 'We shall eat until we cannot stand.' The aesthetics of obesity are widely prized. Among the Banyankole of East Africa, a girl prepares for marriage at about eight years old by staying indoors and drinking milk for a year until corpulence reduces her walk to a waddle.[4] It is striking how the sheer quantity of food served – and sometimes eaten – persists in some societies as an indication of status. Jack Goody, Britain's greatest living anthropologist, has devoted much inconclusive pondering to the problem of why west Africa has never developed a courtly cuisine but continues to rely on big meals as measures of chiefly status. Tribute traditions in this region have enabled chiefs to maintain large households: Chief Gandaa of Biriku, for instance, whose funeral Goody attended, had 33 wives and more than 200 children but, like other chiefs in the region, 'he lived just like everyone else, only with more of everything.' No separate style of cooking or serving is apparent, though chiefs normally have to eat out of public gaze. Among the traditional Yoruba, it was a customary obligation for a king to eat his predecessor's heart and other special ritual foods were prescribed, and in Gonja, in northern Ghana, feasts of yam or cassava with fish or meat relish are laid on under the chief's auspices at rites of passage. But these practices hardly seem to have the makings, or to constitute the potential menu, of a courtly cuisine.[5]

Where does thin come from?

Even in the modern West, until the last century, habits of atavistic over-eating recurred in high-status individuals, even though society had abundant other ways of honouring rank. Pride in big meals and bodily corpulence survived the medieval demonisa-

3 Kemp BJ, 1989, *Ancient Egypt*, Routledge, London, pp 120–8.
4 Powdermaker H, 1997, 'An anthropological approach to the problems of obesity', in C Counihan and P van Esterick (eds), *Food and culture; a reader*, Routledge, New York, pp 203–10.
5 Goody J, 1982, *Cooking, cuisine and class*, Cambridge University Press, Cambridge, pp 40–78.

tion of gluttony in the Middle Ages and the neo-Stoical cult of moderation which was part of the 'civilising process' of the Renaissance and early modern times. Waists were barely slimmed by the nineteenth-century cult of the romantic waif. It is not, perhaps, surprising that revulsion from fat took so long to become normal in our culture. It is a striking reversal of a long-standing evolutionary trend. From a biologist's point of view, the human body can be seen as a startlingly efficient repository for fat, which we secrete in relatively large amounts and deposit more widely around our bodies than any other land mammal. A healthy, normal-sized Western woman today has a body which is, on average, 30 per cent adipose tissue: not even polar bears and penguins can rival that level of attainment.[6] Esteem for fatness was part of the earliest aesthetic we know of: the prejudice in favour of big-hipped, bosomy beauties in Stone Age carvings.

Now, however, the era of esteemed adiposity is over in the West. Obesity is a disqualification for status. The last really fat US president was William Howard Taft, who was so enormous that he could not tie his own shoelaces. Nowadays, that level of obesity would weigh down any political career. Bill Clinton, who was not particularly fat, suffered almost as much obloquy for his slack waistline as for his loose morals. Dieting is now as much de rigueur for politicians as for female entertainers. Big corporations sack the fat and discriminate in favour of the thin in appointments and promotions. The fat are in danger of self-reclassification as a persecuted minority: that, indeed, is the message of the quaintly named 'National Association for the Advancement of Fat Americans'. Obesity has to justify itself as a form of disability, demanding 'equal rights' for fat people: fat-friendly turnstiles, extra-long car seat belts.

Meanwhile, affluence formerly spent on engorgement is wasted, in our society, on the thinning gym. Hostility to fat drives the anxious to anorexia. The thin image is advocated by a thousand publicity campaigns on grounds of beauty, morals and health. A modern mantra is: fat is grim, fit is trim. The historic profile of body fat has undergone a revolution. Historically, poverty has been thin and fatness has been an index of social standing. In today's most developed societies, the rich are thin and obesity is a mark of the underclass.

6 Pond C, 1998, *The fats of life*, Cambridge University Press, Cambridge, pp 1–62, pp 210–23.

The change has been relatively sudden, concentrated in the period since the late nineteenth century.[7] In a little over a hundred years, we've discarded the standards of Rubens and Renoir, and substituted those of Barbie and Twiggy. Most artists of the past would now be classed as fat-fetishist weirdos. No one knows how it happened. Classic explanations blame capitalism and industrialisation: the diet and fashion industries created a market for thinness – an ideal product from the suppliers' viewpoint, a demand which could be infinitely prolonged and never satisfied.[8] There is probably something in this – but fat would surely be more easily saleable. Some feminists blame men for trying to re-craft women's body-shapes.[9] But anti-fat propaganda is not gender specific; female fashion editors and designers connive in its campaigns; and feminism has contributed to the hallowing of women's own bodily 'control', of which dieting is an aspect. Medical wisdom is often credited with effecting the revolution: but the modern demonisation of fat far exceeds anything which could be justified by genuine health concerns. There are fat-related diseases but most fat people do not have them. Roland Barthes is said to have claimed that it was just a matter of fashion:[10] but the preference for fatness over thinness lasted too long to be called fashionable; and its reversal shows no sign of easing.

Really, we are experiencing a cultural revolution with obvious economic roots. As food has cheapened, fatness has become easy to attain. Tempted by an affordable indulgence, the poor over-eat; middle-class moralists condemn them for it as formerly they condemned the corresponding excesses of earlier generations of poor people: tipples at the gin and flutters at the races. The great lesson of the current global obesity 'pandemic' is that urbanisation actually makes it hard for some poor people to stay thin, as rural diets, low in sugar and starch, are replaced by high-energy fixes, preservative-steeped shop-stored comestibles and sneakily fattening 'convenience' foods. 'Food deserts' in modern cities are actually oases of dietary junk.[11]

Running away from the poor

Normally in history, when the cost of culture changes, its social profile changes, too. The rich have to be different. They flee from the practices of the poor. The rich lose their taste for easily

7 Stearns PN, 1997, *Fat history*, SUNY Press, New York.
8 Schwarz H, 1983, *Never satisfied*, Smithmark, New York.
9 Seid RP and Wolff JG, 1989, *Never too thin*, Prentice Hall, New York
10 Klein R, *Eat fat*, 1996, Diane, New York, p 63.
11 See the recent Demos report by Tim Lang.

accessible pleasures. Because aesthetic trends unfold at the command of elites, the rise of the thin aesthetic has matched the decline of the price of food. When thinness became a luxury instead of a common condition, fat was bound to lose face. Something similar has happened with the cult of muscles: when bodily strength was useful, the upper classes affected physical delicacy; now that muscles are useless, they have become an expensive fashion accessory, which – in most of the sedentary occupations favoured by the 'knowledge-economy' – you need time and money to cultivate. So it is with food: as the poor eat more, the rich eat less.

The era of cheap food may not last: indeed, I hope it does not; it is ecologically disastrous, because of the polluting effects of intensive agriculture. Traditional farming would put up our food bills but rescue our environment. At the moment, however, the wealth gap is dividing diets in terms of quality as well as quantity. There is plenty of fodder to fatten on, but well-produced food is in danger of becoming another prerogative of the thinner classes. Our best hope, in the present connection, is for more embourgeoisement of the kind which has already rev-olutionised taste in Britain in recent times and driven so many supermarket staples upmarket: as the thin aesthetic spreads through society, and the fatter classes ape the slimness of the celebs they admire, demand for cheap food will slacken; more people will want less, of higher quality, and – if capitalism works – the market will respond.

Felipe Fernández-Armesto is a Professorial Fellow in History and Geography at Queen Mary and Westfield College, University of London; he is also a member of the Faculty of Modern History of Oxford University. He is the author of Food: A History, *Macmillan, 2001.*

Slow down: the return to local food

Consumer power offers the surest route to preserving diversity within national and local food cultures

Carlo Petrini

Food as an entity, as a mere set of nutritional elements devoid of all other possible connotations, is universally seen as 'body fuel'. Fair enough – that is its primary, natural, irreplaceable function. Food is, of course, necessary for human survival, one of our few truly essential needs. This is why the search for and consumption of food occupy such a large chunk of our time (it's part of our nature). This is also largely why food manages to influence our culture, our history and our habits – so much so that it has become a distinctive trait of relatively large groups of people.

Food is produced from the land, from its fruits, from the animals that live on it. It can be consumed either as it is, or processed by human beings. Besides thinking in terms of our needs, we thus have to consider where food comes from and how it has been treated and kept. In this sense, food has always been the main factor of interaction between human beings and nature, hugely influencing the transformations that people have imposed on their natural environment and the places where they have chosen to settle and work. The sourcing of raw materials prompted people to develop techniques to maximise their use;

this heightened their ingenuity and, over the centuries, allowed them to assimilate a whole baggage of know-how, tricks and discoveries that is now part and parcel of our culture.

Food can also be extremely pleasurable; it is thus necessary to take into account aspects such as choice, methods of preparation, and ways of serving and eating dishes. Every processing technique, every recipe, the various phases and codes of eating, at the table or in the street, by day or by night, have become veritable rites, designed to improve not only economic, political and social situations that have arisen in the course of history, but also the potential pleasurableness of what nature has to offer. Just think of all the precepts the world's various religions have established with regard to the consumption of food. Alternatively – mysticism apart – consider service and preparation in the world's finest restaurants.

All these aspects are interconnected and have helped write a good part of the history of humanity, deciding the outcome of wars, enriching peoples, and accompanying or changing with the great upheavals our world has undergone over the centuries.

It is thus undeniable that food plays a central role in the formation of local cultures, affecting the economic, social and political aspects of the lives of the various populations. It is just as undeniable that such aspects, in turn, influence the way food is produced and consumed. Between the industrial revolution and the ongoing processes of globalisation, the speed with which one technological innovation followed another in agriculture and food production (partly thanks to the development of transport and the computerisation of human activities) has, on the one hand, redefined the relationship between human beings, food and nature and, on the other hand, allowed new standardised models of production and consumption to spread over most of the planet.

The onward march of science and progress

Major radical changes started to take place in agricultural practice just after the end of the Second World War. Huge masses of people were in need of food and better nutrition, but agricultural production was unable to satisfy this demand in terms of both quantity and quality. Governments decided to finance research and development in the agricultural sector, placing the onus on studies aimed at increasing productivity. New techniques, new products, and new hybrids and crossbreeds gradually appeared on the market, giving rise to what we now call intensive agricultural practices. Chemical solutions were found to solve problems of soil fertility and to fight the war against parasites; medical solutions were adopted to increase and speed up the fattening of animals; and *new* varieties of plants and animals appeared capable of sustaining these treatments and supplying larger quantities of food in the briefest time possible. An appropriate example was that of Holstein cattle, specially bred to produce larger quantities of milk than older breeds. The age of biotechnology had begun. The operation proved successful and set in motion a highly profitable industry tied to agronomy and zootechnics, with a few large multinationals holding the patents and developing research to increase productivity. These selfsame industrial groups are now testing, and starting to market, transgenic organisms worldwide.

The urgent need to produce more somewhat overshadowed the costs – in terms of the chemical pollution of soil and water, the progressive replacement and disappearance of autochthonous varieties and breeds, lower food security, and loss of flavour and aroma – of this productive approach.

While this was happening in the fields and farms, food processing was making great strides forward. Faster, safer transport, new food conservation techniques, and the use of additives to modify aroma, taste, texture and colour allowed the food industry to transcend the freshness of ingredients, their seasonal cycles, and their provenance. The industry invented more and more innovative ways of food processing (from the foods of the 50s, deliberately adulterated to conjure up an aura of modernity, to present-day pre-cooked frozen concoctions which are designed to give the appearance of having just come out of a domestic kitchen, thus stressing the freshness and naturalness of their ingredients) whilst at the same time creating new needs in terms of raw material production (the need for products capable of resisting violent processing treatments and meat and vegetables that are as standardised as possible, even if they do come from opposite ends of the globe).

Intensive agriculture and the food industry have managed to

feed millions of people at a low price and have become closely connected – so much so that they now combine to form a single sector. Large-scale retailing in supermarkets and franchise catering have completed the picture, closing the circle from the field and the barn to the consumer, simultaneously thus triggering a whole series of problems which, although initially not considered top priority, have proved decisive and strategic over time.

The casualties of change

What have we lost in our fight to win the postwar battle of hunger? The picture I have painted gives an idea of the production techniques of many of the foods served on our tables today. The Western world now boasts food in abundance. The urgent needs of the postwar years have long been met, but the productive approach has changed very little. Why? The answer is simple: although this approach made food available at a lower price, it was also very profitable for its perpetrators. But what are these foodstuffs that cost less, and are available all year round, all over the world, really like?

They are poorer in terms of taste and aroma because the characteristics of raw materials – the elements that add taste and give pleasure – are destroyed by unnatural chemical treatments and are reconstructed using standardised additives. They are less safe and healthy for our bodies because the centralisation of production techniques may create mass problems of public health. Such foods are completely de-contextualised because they are the fruit of a global industrial culture that has nothing to do with the socio-economic situations in which they are produced and consumed. These are foods that become part of our culture simply because they appear in all their glory in advertising posters.

The modern way of producing food has left a strong mark on the bonds that have been consolidated over centuries between food and local cultures. Standardised industrial food is the identity of a brand, not of a people. The cultivation of raw materials and their transformation are processes that no longer involve consumers, who thus lose their ability to choose and judge food. The countryside has been depopulated and whole fields have been given over to monocultures. Rural communities are progressively becoming inhospitable, polluted environments in which biodiversity is threatened every day. Food traditions risk becoming an anthropological exercise, totally removed from reality.

We have already lost a good deal of biodiversity. The least productive autochthonous animal breeds and vegetable varieties that have been replaced by new crossbreeds and hybrids in many parts of the world have disappeared, or are disappearing, taking with them their special qualities, unique flavours and aromas, specially developed traditional artisan production methods, rites of consumption and recipes tied to the passing of the seasons. We have thus lost cultural diversity, local identity and variety of taste.

Salvage effort

But what *has* been saved and what *can* be saved? The processes I describe are of course common only in some areas of the developed world. Both in Europe (the most depressed areas of the Mediterranean, for example) and in developing countries, what was once considered productive backwardness has allowed us to save at least some of the traditional agricultural and gastronomic practices that combine to form a strong cultural identity. Developing countries where broad sections of the population suffer from problems of poor nutrition are, alas, becoming ideal places to transfer many of the intensive techniques increasingly frowned upon by public opinion in the Western world.

Today, in the wake of food scandals such as 'mad cow disease' and 'dioxin chickens', the average consumer has become much more conscious of the methods of production and origins of food. Until a short time ago, we had the paradox of a few rich farmers producing large quantities of poor-quality food for huge masses of low wage earners, while a few peasants in depressed areas continued to practise quality traditional agriculture for an elite of wealthy consumers. Today we are witnessing the breakdown of this class-based division of Western consumers. On the one hand, we have consumers concerned about the quality of the food they eat (in terms of its wholesomeness, knowledge of production methods, the origin of raw materials, freshness, naturalness and the cultural connotations any artisan product is bound to encapsulate). On the other hand, we have consumers, rich and poor alike, who see food basically as body fuel with no interest in all its other aspects.

It is this second group of consumers with whom we have to share the blame for the persistence of intensive agriculture and a food industry without any care for quality, not to mention the progressive erasure of food's nobler, deeper significance within our society. But it is on the first group of consumers that we have to pin our hopes for at least a partial reorganisation of the agro-industrial sector.

'Shopping bag power' is one of the most effective means by which civil society imposes new methods of food production. Defending breeds, varieties, techniques and products on the verge of extinction is not only a way of promoting an agro-industrial sector using eco-sustainable practices. It is also a way of claiming the right to food pleasure: meaning not only taste but also knowledge. By catering for consumers sensitive to these issues, small economies of scale bound up in local agriculture and the surrounding countryside will demonstrate that they work better than the present system of food production – in every sense. In this way, it will also be possible to safeguard local cultures and identities. Far from being a form of conservatism, all this amounts to a mission to defend every aspect of the complexity and diversity that are the most important values of a world moving towards top-down standardisation. Food is no longer a decisive factor in the formation of distinctive, vibrant local and national cultures; however, it can be a way of defending them, helping them to grow and come to terms with each other in a peaceful way.

Carlo Petrini has been President of Slow Food since July 1986 when the movement was founded in the Italian region of Piedmont. The aim of the movement is to counter the tide of standardisation of taste and the manipulation of consumers around the world. Slow Food now has 65,000 members in 45 countries.

Food is not fuel

We should savour the social side of eating and resist the instant meal

Geraldine Bedell

In his book on *The English*, Jeremy Paxman[1] writes: 'For the majority of people, eating out is to consume fat-filled fast food, and to eat in, to be a victim of something pre-packaged.' Paxman's smug dismissiveness is typical of British food commentary, which often assumes that other people – usually poorer people – don't know what's good for them. The poor, it is implied, have bad diets and only themselves to blame for obesity and ill health. We are presented with so much choice in matters of food that it comes as a relief to have something to reject comprehensively; anxious to feel secure about our own choices, we are eager to rubbish those of others. And there is sufficient truth in the poor-eat-bad-food line to make it a comfortable, easy-to-live-with prejudice.

Yet as the Demos report *Inconvenience Food*[2] suggested, low-income consumers are set apart from the rest of the population, not by ignorance or laziness about cooking or shopping, but chiefly by the difficulty of trying to do the same thing as everybody else, despite the structural obstacles of access, food availability and being both time- and cash-poor. Choice is a luxury of the affluent, as the shelves of Britain's supermarkets testify.

My local Waitrose currently stocks the following potatoes: Romano, Duke of York, King Edward, Estima, Desiree, New

1 Paxman J, 2000, *The English: a portrait of a people*, Overlook Press, New York.
2 Hitchman C et al, 2002, *Inconvenience food: the struggle to eat well on a low income*, Demos, London.

Carlingford, New Maris Piper, Large Grade, Salad, Salad Red, Organic Baking, Organic Large, Organic Red, Organic of no particular specification, Organic New and Organic New Baby. My local LIDL, on the other hand, offers just one kind – Selected. This is significant because, according to the British Potato Council, the British are increasingly consuming potatoes as crisps, chips and ready-to-cook meals. Only 50 per cent of potatoes (of which we eat as many as ever) are bought in their natural state – a shift, it has been suggested, that may be an indicator of increased obesity. And we know that, in rich nations, obesity tends to afflict the urban poor, so it's easy to deduce that the move away from natural foods – foods in their raw state, foods that must be chopped, boiled or baked – is being spearheaded by the poorest consumers. In fact, a comparison of potato availability in Waitrose and LIDL probably tells us no more than this – poorer consumers, as ever, are offered fewer choices.

The curse of convenience

There is nothing new about the poor having a more restricted diet. What is new is a kind of utilitarian attitude to food that cuts across all social classes. Despite our increasing obsession with food – it's hard to open a newspaper without encountering a story about child obesity or problematic ingredients – we may actually be missing the crucial point. It's the things we do through and around food that matter and if only we could concentrate on them, we might actually eat better.

For the majority of us who are not poor (and, according to the Henley Centre, 70% of people in the UK, which includes many people on below-average incomes, never have to worry about budgeting for food) the choice of food has never been greater. This has led to a massive growth in take-up of convenience food, for perfectly understandable reasons: the growth in single-person households; the numbers of women in the workforce; the average 44-hour working week; and the increasing affluence and independence of children. In many homes, family members need to eat at different times, or food has to be rustled up quickly. At the expensive end of the market, pre-marinated meats, washed salads and cut fruit are on offer to ease the process; at the cheap end, the options are similar but less costly and, probably, nastier.

During the week, food tends to be assembled rather than cooked. An overview of recent food research for the British Potato Council found that for many people there was a 30-minute midweek limit for food preparation and 60 per cent of adults view chicken nuggets and baked beans as a home-cooked meal. It also revealed that adult-only households were more likely to cook from primary ingredients, and ready-made sauces were commoner in homes with children. Social class had almost nothing to do with it.

For many people, the range of food currently available offers welcome choice. But there has also been a cost: consumer demand has lead to massive market fragmentation, the most dramatic aspect of which has been the increase in 'grazing'. The market for crisps, snacks and nuts is now worth £1.5 million. When I was a child, it was against school rules to eat in the street in school uniform; today such a prohibition would be incomprehensible. The new multiplex cinema near me has what amounts to a food court in the lobby, and a holder for popcorn and fizzy drinks in every seat. A French acquaintance of mine observed recently that the sandwich barely exists in France, and that – either as a cause or consequence of this – French people don't eat at all times of day. But, here, all the indications are that we are going the way of the US, where 30 per cent of meals are consumed in the car, and the 7–11 foodstore chain has launched a range called 'Dashboard Dining'. Some 47 per cent of British adults now eat their main evening meal in front of the box and consumer research consistently shows that where families do eat together, they do so more around the television than at the table.

All this eating on the move and on the sofa has serious implications. It tends towards an idea of food as fuel, where ease and efficiency are the most important considerations. This instrumental view of food is reinforced by the welter of dietary advice that assaults us on a daily basis. Purveyed by pop nutritionists, often on the basis of research paid for by the food industry, this is utterly bewildering. To take just one example, the formula for linoleic acid is $CH_3(CH_2CHCH)_3(CH_2)_7COOOH$. Most oils and fats contain a dozen or so fatty acids of this kind, and butter has more than 100. It therefore becomes impossible for even an informed and interested non-expert to judge whether the nutritionists are right when they suggest we should give up naturally produced butter, which our ancestors have been enjoying for centuries, in favour of spreads made of hardened vegetable fat with mysterious additives.

Human beings have always had protean, indefinite appetites; our omnivorousness is not a modern problem. Aristotle worried over how to limit instinctive voracity:

> For just as man, when he is perfected, is the best of
> animals, so too, separated from law and justice, he
> is worst of all. . . . Without virtue he is most unholy
> and savage, and worst in regard to sex and eating.

Brillat-Savarin observed, not dissimilarly, that 'beasts feed; man eats; the man of intellect alone knows how to eat.' Sitting down to table requires some commitment to the food, both in its preparation and eating, which is way beyond what happens when you simply raid the refrigerator. Throughout history, in all cultures, tastes have been educated and manners honed through rituals of eating. Not eating with children and not consuming the same food as them around a table is an abdication of responsibility to educate their tastes and teach them civility. (And, additionally, has opened the way for the explosion of child-focused foods, which have immediate taste appeal but actually teach them very little about the range of flavours on offer.)

Social rituals

Leon Kass, Professor of Social Thought at the University of Chicago, argues persuasively in his book *The Hungry Soul*,[3] that rituals that have grown up over centuries around food are of great benefit to us and, as he would put it, help us to 'realise the pointings and yearnings of our nature' – towards community and friendship (through shared meals and hospitality); towards beauty and nobility (through gracious manners and beautiful tables); towards discernment and understanding (through

3 Kass LR, 1999, *The hungry soul: eating and the perfecting of our nature*, University of Chicago Press, Chicago.

tasteful food and lively conversation); and towards the divine (through ritual sanctification of the meal). I wouldn't go all that way, but I think he has a point: we eat better, and more moderately, when we eat with more pleasure.

It doesn't do to be overly nostalgic. While it's true that, at home, we want food to be social while consuming it in ever less social situations, it's also the case that new opportunities for food sociability have arisen. There is far more eating out at restaurants than there used to be and, thanks to the explosion of ethnic food, far more opportunities to share. We may have sat round the table every night when I was a child, but we didn't dip into the same curry, or pass round dishes of Chinese food between us. My teenage children go to coffee bars to read newspapers, send emails and bump into their friends.

Fragmentation of the market for food means, among other things, that affluent areas have seen a return to one-basket High Street shopping, with specialist delicatessens, organic butchers and high-class fishmongers; that there are farmers' markets in country towns and cities, and organic chains like Fresh and Wild; that supermarkets have exclusive sections with premium-priced balsamic vinegars, preserves and porcini. The increase in foreign travel and the extent of immigration has given the UK the most varied food culture of any in Europe. An American friend of mine recently returned from a tour of rural England with his family saying they had mostly eaten curry (appropriately enough, since Robin Cook says chicken tikka masala is the national dish). Meanwhile, in urban areas, the curry house is giving way to Goan, Keralan and Bangladeshi restaurants. It is not unusual for pubs, even country pubs, to serve Thai food and, a couple of years ago, Waitrose introduced a Goan dish called Xacutti, which, at that stage, you would have been hard pressed to find in any British restaurant.

As a woman who likes working, it does not seem to me a bad thing that food has moved away from being the focus of the household to become an adjunct. As a mother, I know how hard it is to get teenage children to turn up for meals and not just throw a jar of sauce onto some pasta because they need to meet their friends *now*. But food is not merely fuel: it is a social glue, an aesthetic experience, a gift to others and an opportunity to respect other people's work. Eating on the run some of the time is fine, but doing it all the time diminishes us. The more stress we suffer, the more we are likely to seek out just-in-time food for our just-in-time lives, which is ultimately bad for our health because we notice less what we are consuming. This brings us back to the poorest consumers, who not only can't afford the organic butchers but lead stressed lives and are often under pressure to feed children food that is immediately palatable. In stress, rather than in ignorance or fecklessness, lies the attraction of convenience foods.

If the government is serious about improving the nation's diet, there is limited value in adding to the often contradictory plethora of nutritional strictures. It *would be* much better to address the culture of food in this country, which is insecure for sound historical reasons. But the Britain of watery cabbage and indeterminate brown meat is over. We actually have fantastic food, and we should be bolder about acknowledging it – making a meal of it. We should celebrate our artisanal producers, as the French do, and glory in our ethnic culinary diversity. Cooking should go back on the school curriculum, not in the old, dreary home economics format, but as a branch of the arts. We should remember that much of what is good about food is the way we eat it. And we may be surprised at the impact it has on all of our anxieties about eating if we think of food primarily as a pleasure.

Geraldine Bedell is a writer for The Observer *and, for most days of the week, a cook.*

The spice of life?

The middle classes appreciate ethnic diversity when they eat out, but that isn't real multiculturalism

David Lammy

Variety's the very spice of life,
That gives it all its flavour.
(William Cowper, *The task*, 1785)

Writing about food is not something I find difficult. As a child, my greatest ambition in life was to become neither a Member of Parliament, nor a lawyer. It was to be successful enough, in whatever I ended up doing, to be able to fill my fridge with food. I remember visiting my elder brother's house for the first time shortly after he was married and being in awe of the quantity and unfamiliarity of the food that lurked behind his fridge door. At home, a full fridge was not something that my mother, a working single parent, could ever have hoped to provide.

But, for me, the significance of food has always been about more than just affluence. Growing up somewhere as diverse as Tottenham, it was clear long before politicians were making speeches about our 'chicken tikka society' that food was a crucial indicator of diversity and cultural richness. It was an integral part of the multiculturalism that I was encouraged to 'celebrate' at that time – what I sometimes call the multicultur-alism of samosas, saris and steel drums – but also of the multi-cultural identity that I was subconsciously creating for myself, by making friends from different backgrounds and spending time in their homes and with their families.

That food has turned out to be the medium through which British multiculturalism has perhaps expressed itself most articulately, and certainly most visibly, is not entirely surprising. As Drew Smith, the former editor of the *Good Food Guide*, has argued, ethnic minority cooking in the 1980s rescued traditional British cuisine from a rather deep rut. But I think, at a deeper level, this also reflects the historic function that food has performed in bringing people together and breaking down the cultural barriers between them. As decades of anthropology research have made clear, the sharing of food is a key step for researchers to gain the trust of the group they are trying to observe. The way we eat (or don't eat) together says a great deal about the character and quality of our relationships, whether within families or within communities.

In this essay, I want to suggest that these three themes – food as identity, food as affluence, and food as cohesion – are closely linked by a common thread: that politics has not yet managed to develop a coherent response to the opportunities and challenges of diversity.

Food and British identity

At first glance, things look pretty good. Britain's food culture, for so long a national embarrassment, is now a growing source of national pride. Multiculturalism has been central to that renaissance. Before the Italians and Greeks, Chinese and Thai, and Bangladeshis and Indians came to Britain, bringing their food with them, eating out was just another elitist British institution. The pomp and ceremony of unpronounceable French dishes and intricately laid tables were a substitute for a genuinely shared food culture to which more than just the wealthy could relate. Multiculturalism helped to unsettle that old order and, for the first time, made restaurants accessible to the many, not the few.

The prominence of food within a wider popular culture has also risen dramatically. Food was a recurring theme of the 'cool Britannia' optimism that characterised the late 1990s. On a personal level, I felt this transformation particularly acutely upon returning to Britain after several years of studying and working in the United States. On TV, for example, food and cookery programming had diversified beyond the staid format popularised by Delia Smith. Jamie Oliver was the exemplar of a new breed of media personality – the 'celebrity chef' – who could communicate with young as well as old and convince a new generation that food could be fun. What made this new style of cookery so exciting and inspiring was the multiculturalism of the recipes: giving traditional British cuisine a make-over by fusing different gastronomic cultures and traditions, taking the best from each to create something that reflected the unique character of British multi-ethnicity. As top chef Peter Gordon recently put it, 'Britain is the country where my European friends feel the most excited by the diversity available.'[1]

One of the most tangible expressions of how eloquently food can encapsulate the potential of diversity is Rusholme in Manchester. On the map, the main street through Rusholme is Wilmslow Road, but to anyone who has been there, it is the 'curry mile'. Some of the finest curry restaurants in the country sit side by side with only their vividly coloured neon signs to differentiate them, giving the unsuspecting visitor the sensation that they have stumbled upon a little piece of Las Vegas in the heart of South Manchester. This is picture-postcard multiculturalism. It is inclusive: visit any of these restaurants and one cannot help but be struck by the diversity of its clientele. At one table sits an Asian family, at the next an elderly white couple, at another a group of rowdy students. It contributes to the city's identity, helping to shape the vibrant municipal culture that Manchester has recreated for itself over the last decade. And it is good for the economy: the chefs and waiters who prepare and serve the food are among the estimated 70,000 people employed in curry restaurants nationally.[2] One of the proprietors in Rusholme has even diversified into production, and her restaurant-branded curry sauce can now be found in supermarkets up and down the country.

Divided by diet

Unfortunately, my own constituency of Tottenham is not a jewel in London's gastronomic crown the way that Rusholme is in Manchester's. At lunchtime on Seven Sisters Road, I do not

1 Gordon P and Skidelsky W, 2002, *Prospect* magazine, November.

2 Leonard M, 1997, *Britain™: Renewing our identity*, Demos, London.

see my constituents emerging from chic ethnic restaurants or Bohemian cafés. Instead I see them pouring out of chip shops and Kentucky Fried Chicken clones, a homogenised fast food façade that conceals and ignores the diversity of the local community beyond it. When I shop at my local supermarket, the exotic fruit and vegetables that fill the shelves at their Earl's Court store are conspicuous by their absence. In their place are 'two for the price of one' offers on processed foods that provide cheap calories but not always much in the way of nutritional value. And at my monthly surgeries, many of the constituents who come to me with the most desperate problems have bad diet written all over their faces. It is rarely their main concern, but that itself is part of the problem: whatever our income, it seems none of us have time to worry about nutrition. For those of us who can páy for it, food retailers have come up with all sorts of ways of preparing healthy food quickly. But this convenience comes at a cost many of my constituents cannot afford. In Tottenham, as elsewhere, we are divided by diet, not united by it.

It is not that Tottenham is any less diverse than Rusholme – on the contrary, mine is the most diverse constituency in Europe. At the most recent estimate, 193 languages are spoken there.[3] Behind each, I am willing to bet, there are recipes, techniques and ingredients that make up a unique food culture every bit as rich as those that have already taken root in mainstream British society. The problem is that this tacit social knowledge is not put to use in any meaningful way. Instead it is locked away behind the doors of people's homes, denied public expression by their poverty and by their exclusion from participating in, and interacting with, the local community. Imagine the incredible creative fusions that could flow if this private diversity could be articulated within a shared public arena.

That such a resource has been so scandalously untapped is unfortunately an apt metaphor for the plight of my constituents in other respects. Their language skills and tacit cultural know-how, not to mention their international networks of contacts, could be tremendously valuable to wider society in a range of ways.[4] But this wealth of talent and experi-

3 http://www.haringey.
gov.uk/data/abouthar/
factfile.asp
4 Lammy D, 2002,
'Rediscovering interna-
tionalism', in P Griffith
and M Leonard (eds)
Reclaiming Britishness,
Foreign Policy Centre,
London.

ence is too often wasted because it is not captured in the form of a currency that the labour market can understand. My constituents are prevented from benefiting from the rich diversity that surrounds them because they are deprived of the basic means and resources, which are a precondition for even the most elementary forms of social participation. They deserve to share much more than their social exclusion; they must certainly share more than chips and fried chicken.

This is the main problem with the idea of multiculturalism as it has been understood up till now. It sees diversity as an end in itself rather than as a way of widening our range of choices about how we live our lives. And as Bauman has argued, 'any serious defence of the intrinsic value of the variety of cultural choice needs to start from securing the degree of human self-esteem and self-confidence that makes such choices possible.'[5] In other words, the flaw in the multicultural heaven is that the chorus sings with a middle-class accent.[6]

Food and politics

So what is the role for politics in responding to these challenges? Invoking a classical liberal position, many argue that personal choices about the food we eat are made in a private sphere on which politics has no right to encroach. If these choices have unfortunate personal consequences for individuals' well-being, then so be it.

But this account is flawed in three major respects. First, it is clear that these individual choices have collective consequences, not least in terms of the additional burden they place on the NHS. It is widely accepted, for example, that some of the main causes of premature death in the UK, including coronary heart disease, diabetes and several common forms of cancer, are directly linked to the excess consumption of fat and under-consumption of fruit and vegetables. Second, it is also clear that in many cases these 'choices' are not really choices at all. As a recent Demos report argued, low income, lack of transport, the pressures of single parenthood and the nature of modern food retailing are all factors in the growing prevalence of 'food poverty': a form of social exclusion which robs people of the right to 'choose' a nutritious diet.[7]

5 Bauman Z, 2001, 'Whatever happened to compassion?', in T Bentley and D Stedman Jones (eds) The moral universe, Demos, London.
6 cf. Schnattschneider E, 1975, The semi-sovereign people, Harcourt Brace Jovanovich, London.
7 Hitchman C et al, 2002, Inconvenience food: the struggle to eat well on a low income, Demos, London.

However, third, and most important, the classical liberal position drastically underestimates the significance of food as a way of bringing people together and also, therefore, its potential usefulness as a tool within wider strategies for promoting social inclusion. As government searches for new ways to engage people in areas like Tottenham – to support them in their efforts to succeed in the labour market or the education system, to develop their capacity for shared action and to overcome their prejudices, fears and insecurities – food can and should be a crucial resource.

Linking together the patchwork of fragmented, half-remembered, as well as the more well-established, food cultures that exist in Tottenham and elsewhere would be a powerful illustration of the possibilities of social cohesion. A common food culture, in which we can all engage, even if not on entirely equal terms, would help to build shared cultural experiences and promote intercultural understanding. But it would also help to uncover forms of social and economic knowledge and potential that too often remain hidden from view. I know from my own experience that some of the best food in Tottenham is served up in the many community centres run by and for different sections of the area's diverse population. However, apart from me, few people outside those communities get to try it. And the same is true of all the other services they provide, from after-school or holiday clubs to care for the elderly. If multiculturalism is to mean anything, it must break out of these silos. Perhaps food is a good place to start.

In sum, food encapsulates the promise of diversity, but also its perils. It can bring us together, or divide us. And in places like Tottenham, it can be a route to shared identity and understanding or yet another form of social exclusion and division.

If we are looking for causes for optimism, it is that people of my generation may be more prepared than most to accept that food is about more than just individual choice. Indeed, food has a global symbolic resonance for us going back to the 1980s and the success of BandAid in waking up the West to the horrors of famine in Africa. We remember being shocked by the television footage of starving children in Ethiopia and the realisation that millions of people were going without food every day. Food and famine unleashed a latent internationalism in my generation the same way that nuclear weapons and the Vietnam War had in our parents' generation.

Today, food still lies at the heart of the most perverse illustrations of global inequality. As 1.3 billion people struggle to survive on less than a dollar a day in the developing world,[8] there are millions in the West (including many in Britain) who are dying from eating too much and too unhealthily. As their populations starve, developing countries concentrate on growing crops for export so that consumers thousands of miles away can enjoy fruits and vegetables out of season.

So, as we look to develop a new and more inclusive food culture, we must hold foremost in our minds the classic globalisation imperative to act local but think global. In Britain, and beyond, variety can be the spice of life. But the lives we are spicing require some more basic ingredients first.

David Lammy is MP for Tottenham and Parliamentary Under-Secretary of State for Health.

[8] http://www.world bank.org

Social service

Eating out is immensely popular but designing a good restaurant requires the right ingredients

Terence Conran

There are many factors that have caused a huge increase in the number of restaurants, brasseries, bistros, cafés, clubs and bars in cities and towns throughout the world. The main one, I believe, is that because we now spend so much time in front of a screen (whether at the office, in a cinema, at home or, soon, on our mobile phones), we have had to create new opportunities for contact. Café culture allows us to meet, talk, smile, snarl, touch, flirt, kiss or punch real people. It allows us to meet, socialise, discuss, debate and argue.

Whilst interaction, both physical and mental, is probably the single most important reason for the growth of café culture, we are also now much more aware of the value and quality of our spare time. We have less of it available, and therefore we calculate the time taken going to the shops, preparing a meal and cleaning up afterwards, and measure this against the cost of a relaxing meal in a restaurant. We also consider how tired both our partners and we feel at the end of a long working day and question whether we can face the journey home in the rush hour.

We usually enjoy our meals in restaurants and our spirits are raised by a drink in a bar. To most people, this is still an affordable luxury and is seen as a treat but, to many people, frequent dining out has now become a regular way of life. In Manhattan, for instance, many new apartments don't have proper kitchens, only a microwave and a kettle. However, in a contrary development resulting from current concerns about personal safety, others have become more domesticated, and seek comfort and security by cooking at home rather more than they used to. This may be a trend that will develop as we become increasingly threatened by terrorism. The fear of random violence may not only inhibit our movement, and our desire to visit communal social spaces, it may also reinforce the psychological comfort of staying close to the hearth. But in spite of these growing fears, restaurants continue to flourish. Why?

Obviously, the food on your plate is the single most important reason you go to a restaurant and the range of variety, quality and price levels now on offer is enormous. In London, New York, Hong Kong, Sydney, Tokyo or San Francisco, you can eat food from every corner of the world, and even Paris is catching up. At the same time as the world is apparently getting smaller, people's tastes and desires for different regional foods expand, although after spending a week in Tokyo eating nothing but Japanese food, I come home longing for a steak and chips.

It is this huge variety of different foods at different price levels in different environments that has made the café culture so magnetically attractive to so many people. You can only buy what you are offered and how do you know that you might want it until you are offered it? This is a truism that particularly applies to restaurants and is another reason why they have multiplied at such a fast rate in recent years in all the world's centres of population. Diversity and variety of food on offer have promoted growth in the number of places to consume it.

Are you being served?

In choosing a restaurant, service follows hard on the heels of food. Even the best food on your plate or the most charming environment can be ruined by rude, sloppy or arrogant service. In this country, we have not naturally been at ease while waiting on a table. Somehow we have seen it as being below our status. This, thank goodness, is changing and for several reasons.

First, because the restaurant business is now perceived as a modern, entrepreneurial activity and has become an increasingly lucrative place to work. Second, because the common market has allowed professional staff from continental Europe to work in UK restaurants and cafés. This has demonstrated to our nationals how to do the job properly and what a good and pleasant job it can be. Third, because restaurants and hotels have realised that they have to train their staff if they are going to succeed in business.

Fourth, modern technology has helped to make the jobs of the waiters and chefs far easier and more efficient by the use of touch-screens that allow the customers' orders for food and drinks to be whizzed to the kitchen, bar or servery, printed out clearly and assembled into a bill by another touch of the screen. Finally, I think that our decision to open as many kitchens as possible for viewing by customers has removed the war zone that allowed waiters or front of house staff to engage in battle with the chefs and back of house staff.

It is now rare to see waiters leaving the kitchen with a scowl on their face and burnt fingers. We all know what a pleasure it is to be served by a cheerful smiley waiter or waitress, who is not intrusive but attentive, senses what you need before you even realise it yourself and gives you the bill when you ask for it. That is why I would always put service a firm second in importance behind the quality of the food on your plate.

However, a meal in a restaurant in the evening is not just about eating and meeting. It is also seen as an alternative to going to the cinema or a concert or to the theatre, opera or ballet. It is a form of entertainment and a spectator sport, rather than just a way of satisfying your hunger. And, for this reason, the restaurant has to be a very different place from the dining rooms of the past, and the considerations of restaurateurs have to extend well beyond food and service into interior design, lighting, fashion and other areas.

Eating by design

The design of the restaurant is extremely important. Everything in this world that has ever been made by man or woman has to a lesser or greater extent been designed. I am constantly disappointed that 'design' and 'designer' have become such negative, sneer words in common parlance. You hear things described as designer drugs, designer babies, designer food and water, even designer diplomacy. Why? I suppose because people feel let down by the many things they see as over-designed or unintelligently designed, or designed superficially or purely cosmetically.

The design of a restaurant, café or bar is complex and the first imperative is to make it work well for both the staff and the customers. The design features and equipment take an enormous beating from the hardworking kitchen staff, and the customers believe that the chairs, tables and lavatories belong to them but don't treat them with any proprietorial respect, and neither do the cleaners.

The first job of restaurant designers is to make the place function properly and withstand the slings and arrows of outrageous customers and staff. They then have to make the place comfortable and attractive, a place that raises the spirits, a place in which customers feel relaxed and happy.

Designers have to worry about the quality of the air and how cool or warm it is. They have to think hard about the lighting and how it changes from day to night and from season to season. They have to plan how the waiters serve your food and drink and how to make you and your neighbours feel comfortable. They have to consider the level of noise that is appropriate to the type of restaurant it is.

All the details matter: the type of cutlery, china, glass, linen, flowers, the colour, texture and, of course, durability of absolutely everything. Much of it gets broken or stolen and the designers' decisions will affect the amount that this happens.

Running a restaurant, café, bar or club is immensely hard work and, these days, because of increasing EU and national regulations, it is also an expensive project to construct. Nevertheless, there seems to be an insatiable desire amongst entrepreneurs to open new places.

It is partially, I believe, because food culture is seen as an attractive and lucrative activity by creative, young people leaving school and university. Careers in the food industry are now seen in the same way that hairdressing, fashion, photography, advertising, pop music, design and architecture, the law, merchant banking and social services have been seen as the hot, new, attractive careers over the past 40 years or so.

The reason why so many restaurants fail in their first few years is because a lot of knowledge, skill, experience, tenacity and dedication is required to run a restaurant successfully and profitably. This does not easily equate with the ambitions of the leisure generation to work a 35-hour week and be unencumbered by large dollops of bureaucracy designed, as it often appears, to stultify their entrepreneurial enthusiasm.

However, when all goes well, running a restaurant is one of the most exciting careers anybody could wish for – every meal is a new performance, every day a new act.

Sir Terence Conran is a renowned designer, restaurateur and retailer. He founded the Habitat chain of stores, is chairman of Conran Holdings, the parent company of the retail and restaurant businesses, and also chairman of Conran and Partners, his architecture and design practice.

On the menu: why more choice isn't better

The use of menu selection from restaurants to computers is a way of limiting our choices

Rebecca L Spang

When the Treaty of Amiens (1802) interrupted the Napoleonic Wars for 14 months, it was the first time in nearly 10 years that curious Britons had been able to visit Paris safely. Eager to witness the effects of the French Revolution begun in 1789, travellers flocked across the Channel; keen to have their discoveries known, they published volume after volume promising 'a true picture' of remarkable changes and upheavals. In the eyes of many of these visitors, the revolution in French political structures and governing regimes had been mimicked by one in eating habits; among the wonders of Napoleon's Paris – which included the newly opened Louvre museum and the recently acquired Egyptian obelisk – restaurants ranked near the top of the list. Where once, only a few decades ago, the visitor had either to depend on the monotonous, sometimes hardly salubrious, fare of inns and taverns or to rely on the kind invitations of his generous French friends, now he (and, even, she) had dozens, if not hundreds, or perhaps thousands, of restaurants from which to choose.

Purveyors of notionally 'restorative' broths (hence their name), the first self-styled restaurateurs had actually opened their doors in the 1760s. They had also developed a new framework for semi-public eating: small tables, open mealtimes and printed menus all marked a dramatic break from the table d'hôte service that had been the norm across Western Europe.[1] Yet these facts were almost irrelevant to both sceptical Britons and self-congratulatory Frenchmen who easily overlooked the first restaurants in their eagerness to trace this emerging cultural institution to the political changes wrought by the 1789 Revolution. For the British, the splendour and variety offered by Paris's nineteenth-century restaurants proved that France remained a land of extremes (revolution or no), a place where the imperatives of lavish public display ran roughshod over simple common sense. Yet, for French writers like Madame Récamier's lawyer cousin, Jean Anthelme Brillat-Savarin, restaurants offered evidence of the democratisation of French cultural life.[2] No longer the personal possession of comparatively few aristocrats, French haute cuisine was now, thanks to restaurants, available to all.

Infinite variety

In the following decades, Anglo-American travellers would identify restaurants as among the French capital's most distinctive features. Restaurants featured prominently in descriptions of Paris (and, by extension, France) as a place of consumption without production, of prodigality without constraint – a theme developed most fully, perhaps, in discussion of restaurant menus. Presented with a list of seemingly countless dishes, restaurant patrons in the first half of the nineteenth century wrote of 'infinite' variety and considerable bewilderment. Faced with a folio sheet packed with tiny type, travelogue writers were often reduced to ineffective spluttering. Some stunned visitors attempted to quantify their amazement by simply counting the items listed on a restaurant's menu; others saw fit to reproduce a menu's entire text in the pages of their own books. People were often too confused to choose.

The gastronomic vocabulary of restaurant menus perplexed even the most educated and multilingual of voyagers. Today, detailed, sometimes paragraph-long, descriptions may explain a restaurant's specialities and transform its menu into a

1 See my book, *The invention of the restaurant: Paris and modern gastronomic culture*, 2000, Harvard University Press, Cambridge MA.
2 Brillat-Savarin JA, 1825, Le *Physiologie du goût*, currently available in several English translations as *The physiology of taste*.

miniature cookbook, so that a dish is not called by some proper, effectively non-referential, name but is referred to largely as a list of ingredients. We are increasingly familiar with menus that offer abbreviated recipes ('fillets of outdoor-reared, organic pork, served in a mustard, pepper and apple-brandy cream sauce with rocket mash and baby beets') rather than proper names (porc normand). Dish titles have become less allusive, more referential, and the distance between dining-room and kitchen has become shorter rather than longer. But in early nineteenth-century Paris, neither menus nor waiters were so very forthcoming with details of preparation. And perhaps nobody sitting in an ornate salon really wanted to hear from what the ragoût mêlé à la financière (literally, 'financier's mixed stew') had been composed. The grand restaurant promised reliability. The customer had no need to know what was happening in the kitchen, for the restaurant itself stood as the guarantor of uniform quality.

The conventions structuring this new institution had repeatedly to be explained: well into the 1830s, guidebook writers thought it necessary to specify that readers could predict the cost of their restaurant meal simply by reading the menu (and that they need not pay for their dinner until after they had finished eating it). Helpful though these pointers no doubt proved, it was only the first step in understanding. For the menu – so called because it presented a small (menu), summary account of a restaurant's bounty – was much more than a list of foods and prices. An identifying characteristic of any place called a 'restaurant' (as opposed to an inn, tavern, café, or chophouse), the menu remained a far from self-evident technology. One popular cautionary tale of Paris urban mythology indicated that even people who knew how to read could nevertheless be menu illiterates: in the early 1830s, the story has it, a family of provincials went to dine in one of the capital's numerous restaurants. Uneducated in the ways of this still comparatively new and cosmopolitan sociocultural form, the country people ordered one of each item on the menu, and quickly gave up – satiated after seven soups.[3] The rustics, operating with a different classification scheme and treating the carte as a banquet (rather than a restaurant) menu, perceived

3 de Kock P, 1834, 'Les Restaurants et les cartes des restaurateurs', in *Nouveau tableau de Paris au XIXe siècle*, vol 4, Charles Bechet, Paris, pp 82–3.

not categories of interchangeable foods but a set of instructions to be obeyed. Rather than ordering from the menu, the restaurant illiterates were ordered by it.

Portion control

Restaurants (and the menus I take to be among their most distinctive features) both depend upon, and make possible, a particular understanding of selection. For many of us living in Western Europe and North America, restaurant-going has become so routine that we may rarely, if ever, stop to consider what a highly specialised form of public eating it represents. Yet, by their emphasis on discrete units – separate tables, individual portions, distinct menu items – restaurants participate in a worldview that is notably individualistic. Seated at his or her 'own' table, conversing with his or her own friends, eating his or her own dinner, the restaurant patron goes into a social setting in order to avoid dealing with the many other people who are found there.

Conscious efforts have been made to export this format. For instance, a 1961 report to the United States Department of Commerce argued that North American tourism to the Pacific would increase (and, hence, the threat of communism decrease) if there were more à la carte, ie menu-bearing and individual-oriented, restaurants in Indonesia and the Philippines (and more fruity drinks in Fiji).[4] Though not always such an explicit point of deliberate policy, similar assumptions about the effectively private nature of public eating – and, perhaps, of consumer choice in general – have spread widely since 1945.[5]

Now a feature of public eateries in many parts of the globe, menus are also a part of the very technology by which I write this essay. (Desiring to keep my first draft, I pull down the File menu and select 'Save As'.) Should we therefore conclude that eating and computing around the world have been democratised, that choices once open only to elites – be those 14 preparations of veal or 200 fonts – are now widely and wonderfully available to many ordinary people?

Perhaps so, but not without certain costs. One cost is quite literal: as even Brillat-Savarin admitted, a restaurant's open-door admission policy never intentionally extended to serving

4 Clement H, 1961, *The future of tourism in the Pacific and Far East*, US Department of Commerce, Washington DC, June.
5 On this, see my article, 'All the world's a restaurant', 1999, in R Grew (ed) *Food in global history*, Westview, Boulder CO.

those who could not, or would not, pay for their meal. In comparison with the exclusive gentlemen clubs of Victorian London, the famous restaurants of nineteenth-century Paris were markedly public establishments. Yet, if they were public in the sense of being open to all willing buyers, they were never public in the sense of being genuinely shared or communal premises. When the word 'restaurant' was eventually used to refer to such establishments, the 'British Restaurants' set up during the Second World War, for example, it was with the hope that the word's aura of privilege and privacy would enhance the reputation of the government-sponsored canteens.

Another, more paradoxical, cost is the imposition of greater limitation and homogenization. If we can have anything on the menu, we are also usually limited to only those items on the menu. For instance, in my current version of Microsoft Word, it is as impossible to change my page size from the Format menu, as it is easy to do so from the File/Page Setup menu. Menu-structured decision-making may expand our horizons of choice, but it first obliges us to pick a menu. This inherently limits the range of choices that we can make. If many take-away establishments include a sentence on their menus to the effect that 'Chef can prepare on order any dish that is not mentioned in the list,' that ostensible offer of the world on a platter also demands that the patron and chef agree on what constitutes a 'dish'.

A menu is a summary of possible choices. An ample menu – whether it lists soups, wines, or font sizes – specifies by means of omission. A menu omits all the difference that has not been named, all the variation and variability that have not been marked as constituting any particular identity. Long experience with menus encourages us to think of choice as a matter of picking between discrete and distinct entities: saag paneer or saag aloo (even, perhaps, if we are feeling greedy, saag paneer and saag aloo). Menus thereby reinforce the belief in, and search for, the Platonic essences of (or, the 'genuine' recipes for) 'saag paneer' and 'saag aloo' even as they discourage us from imagining the many other ways in which spinach, potatoes and cheese might be, indeed, very frequently have been, combined.

If the word 'menu' has been most widely adopted within the

computer and information-technology industries, we can nonetheless see the menu's basic logic operating in many other aspects of public life today. Take, for example, university degrees. In order to use the same (very limited) resources in order to offer a larger number of degree courses, a university must delimit those degree courses very narrowly. Two different Master's degrees within a given faculty may be allowed to share some course units, but it will also be expected that each has some designated 'core' (of units, seminars, or lectures) that is specific to it alone. Much as the restaurateur who wants to sell both saag paneer and saag aloo must carefully guard against the introduction of potatoes into the former, so the Biology Department with a Biomedical Sciences degree must keep the single-honours Biochemistry students out of the anatomy courses.

Personal choice

All users of a given menu face identical choices; yet they perceive this interaction to be a personal, rather than a collective, matter. We all confront the same options (our files may be new, opened, or closed; our juice may be orange, apple, or tomato) but we normally do so in a manner that individuates rather than unites. We 'personalise' our 'options' much more often than we protest at the choices offered.

In the past decade, 'choice' has been an assumed good in many areas of public policy: education, health care, transport. Yet, consideration of the growth, spread and development of menu-driven selection in multiple arenas should make us at least somewhat wary of this assumption. Arguments that rest on the notion of 'freedom of choice' have inevitably already excluded many other possibilities.

Rebecca L Spang is a historian at University College London. Her book The Invention of the Restaurant: Paris and Modern Gastronomic Culture *has recently appeared in Japanese translation. She is currently interested in money.*

Part 2

Food politics, risk and trust

Hot potatoes: politicians, food and risk

Politicians are always under pressure to reassure the public but they should be honest about risk and the food we eat

John Gummer

From the most sacred to the most trivial of symbols: from bread and wine in the Catholic mass to carrots and sherry for Santa Claus, food plays a central part in the liturgies of life; it has always been pivotal in the world's religions, and its symbolic potency is a factor even in today's world politics. The US finds its trade relationships bedevilled by the Japanese mystic view about rice and its connection with the homeland. I learned round the table of the EU Fisheries Ministers that salted cod is political dynamite in Portugal – a shortage at Easter would seriously undermine a minister's career!

To think that there is something new or surprising about the public's present concern about food is to miss the point. It is not just that food is a practical necessity; it plays a psychological and spiritual role too, even in a deeply secular society. So it is that organic food speaks to us of innocence and nature, of simplicity and purity. The premium is the price we pay for signing up to virtue. Never mind the food miles – much of it comes from halfway round the world – or that farmers can cover it with copper sulphate but never add a teaspoon of potassium. Organics are fulfilling an age-old need to respond to food's spiritual dimension.

Food faddists, vegetarians, vegans and weight watchers provide the liturgy. In rich societies where such choices are easily made, more and more people give point to their daily lives through the rules that such regimens impose upon them. They take control through refusing this and preferring that; through abstention and fasting, they 'detoxify' their bodies and purify their blood. By abominating meat and glorifying pulses, they give a moral dimension to their need to eat.

And they are missionary too. They tell us how much better we would feel if only we gave up bread and all cereals. What a release it is to abstain from alcohol, or chocolate, or dairy products. How many pounds they have lost and what virtue they have won in their quest for perfection. With that zeal goes the usual intolerance. Vegetarians expect the infidels to provide special meals for them but will never turn to and produce them a juicy chump chop. You eat lentils and like it! They are, after all, sure that it is good for you. The moral dimension of their chosen fashion of eating is central.

All of this is not new, it is merely today's response to what seems to be a universal need to link food with the much deeper and more complex concerns of the human spirit. The one significant difference is that this is a version attuned to a rich society. It is the well fed who are able to be picky. Today most of our population has the most extensive choice of food, offered more cheaply and more abundantly than at any previous time. Even so, it is among the most comfortably off that food concerns are most prevalent. We need the leisure, the means and the education to choose organics, avoid beef, excoriate junk food, or exclude GM ingredients. No wonder that, right or wrong, these are the obsessions of the chattering classes.

This is not to minimise these concerns but merely to put them into context. It is a context made more complex by our ever-increasing ability not just to manipulate, but to analyse and detect. We know so much more about our food and our health. We can find the most minute traces of pesticides or additives. The freedom of academia and the drive for research funds give rise to a bewildering number of seemingly science-based claims and counter claims. The media's consciousness of the peculiar resonance of food makes all this the ready stuff of campaigning.

Food will continue to be high on the political agenda. No mere renaming of the Ministry of Agriculture or creation of a Food Standards Agency will satisfy the continuing interest and concern about food issues. Yesterday it was BSE, *Salmonella*, *Listeria* and *E* numbers. Today it is genetically modified organisms (GMOs), battery cages and food miles. Tomorrow it will certainly be obesity as well as a whole new crop of campaigns and scandals. Food will continue to be a high-profile political issue.

The importance of being honest

All this means that we shall need to learn a lot from our past experience. First, transparency is the sine qua non. Naturally, no-one will really believe that ministers tell all they know. That is too far outside the stereotype. All the same, that is what they must do. It is the only proper way to act and, incidentally, the only effective defence in a world where new information is coming in all the time. Ministers have to make decisions on the best evidence they have. They cannot presuppose what may be discovered. They must, instead, take what the scientists can tell them, err wholly on the side of prudence, give everyone all the evidence they have, and then act decisively. That is the hard lesson of the handling of the BSE crisis recognised by the Philips Report.

Openness is, of course, no excuse for inaction. Ministerial sharing of information does not mean the sharing of responsibility. Ministers have to give a lead. They will not be effective in doing so unless people know that what they say is what they really believe, and what they believe informs their actions. If they won't eat beef they can hardly expect the public to believe they think it safe. There is, of course, no guarantee of infallibility, but there ought to be certainty of integrity.

Just as transparency must not become the excuse for inaction, it must not be used to justify delay. If only we had acted decisively in that first fortnight on foot-and-mouth. The British system is proud that consultation and engagement avoid precipitate or high-handed executive action but they can serve too as a mechanism for avoiding necessary emergency decisions. Food crises need immediate action if the confidence of the public is not to be lost. The trick that has to be turned is to ensure that those emergency actions are time limited and do not automatically become the basis for permanent regulation.

I remember that Margaret Thatcher used to go around reassuring the public that we had enacted 19 measures to combat *Salmonella*. I followed behind, knowing that I was busy trying to rescind or drastically modify 18 of them. What had seemed right at the time of the disaster was wholly inappropriate in the long term.

The limits of information

Yet, if ministers do act decisively, on the best available advice, demonstrating their integrity, they can only get it as right as the information available to them allows. Although, in matters of food, the public demands certainty, science cannot provide it. Ministers, on the other hand, are expected to reassure when reassurance is well founded. The public demands that assurance in terms of absolutes – terms that no scientist recognises.

The present government has faced that in dealing with GMOs. I too share the environmentalist concern but there really is nothing to suggest any risk from eating the food. However, no scientist will give an absolutely unconditional clean bill of health. For them, there is nothing that is risk free. That leaves ministers with a very real problem. They know all too well that few among the population have any appreciation of the nature of risk. In those circumstances, what is at issue is the communication of truth.

The fact is that we know that no human activity is risk free and, in common parlance, we pass on information to one another taking that for granted. In public statements, that course is not open to ministers. The only thing they can properly do, therefore, is to show by example what is their own understanding of the best information they have. So, during the *Salmonella* scare, the proper course for ministers would have been to show that they and their families continued to eat eggs but didn't give them to their aged relatives. Nothing would more properly have expressed the truth as presented by the best advice at the time. Spin and semantics have no place in reassurance.

Yet, when the argument is not just about safety, but concerns deeper psychological issues, then the ministerial problem becomes significantly greater. That's why GMOs cause such difficulty. Despite the phrase 'Frankenstein foods' the issue is not safety but 'purity' – a wholly different concept. The government is therefore faced with a campaign that is essentially unsatisfiable. It is made the more so because, although the only real issue is environmental, the popular fear is about food and the argument is carried on in the supermarkets.

GMOs have also served as a focus for resentment about US hegemony and worry about globalisation. The disgraceful behaviour of Monsanto, the unwillingness to label, the insistent use of US political power and the threat of the World Trade Organisation (WTO) have done much to sharpen the debate. They have also highlighted the difference between the European view of food, which reflects many traditional values, and the US commodity approach. They have revealed that in this, as in so much else, the UK is European rather than Atlanticist.

Principled policies

There is a sense in which we do not trust the science, not just because we instinctively believe that it is not always right, but also because we share the feeling that food is not just a matter of science. There are cultural and even spiritual considerations that cannot be ignored. The GMO controversy has reminded us again how complex is our attitude to food. Indeed, the argument here has now recrossed the Atlantic and the public there is beginning to ask the same questions and reveal the same deep concerns, to the consternation of the US multinationals.

All this puts the politician in a hole. It was easy for me to turn back the first shipments of GM maize because the US was pulling a fast one and had not got authorisation. Successive ministers have been able to shelter behind the debates in the EU and the necessity for environmental testing. They are running out of interim excuses and, sooner or later, they will have to make some principled decisions. Are we prepared to go beyond the science, uphold an extension of the precautionary principle and continue to exclude these products? That would make it impossible in the future to stand foursquare on the best available advice argument. Whereas there is just enough scientific concern to stop the use of these products in farming, there is none that would justify banning imports of food products. We would be doing that to protect our farmers from the consequences of an environmental ban upon their competitiveness. A proper subject for the WTO if ever I heard one.

Now, there are many in the scientific establishment who would be horrified at this. Indeed, there is an obvious danger. Ministerial decisions can become arbitrary and ultimately indefensible. Yet, in a democracy, there is a real problem with the insistence that the dictates of world trade (and that, for many, means the dictates of the US) should override the concerns of the customer. It is all too easy for people to feel powerless when, even though their view has majority support, it is the WTO that must rule unchallenged. In these very sensitive issues of food, it is wise for any minister to step warily.

The problem is made more difficult by the legal realities here in the UK. When I was seeking to take decisions on BSE, I was constantly aware that, if I strayed too far from the science, I could be challenged successfully in the courts. Ministers in this country are not beyond the law. We have no concept of special administrative codes that enable ministerial decisions to go unchallenged. So, for example, I couldn't ban the use of fishmeal in animal feed, even though I'd never seen a cow fishing! There was no scientific backing for the contention and, therefore, I would have gone down without any prospect of success. The fact that such a ban would have been environmentally excellent because it would have struck a heavy blow against industrial fishing made the legal prohibition all the more irksome.

Forecasting the food agenda

So it is that food issues will continue to challenge ministers in a high-profile way. We have seen only the early stages of the conflict between food as a commodity and food as something special, produced in a traditional way and playing a particular cultural role. Can feta cheese still be called feta when it is made in Denmark from cow's milk? Are eco-labels on food contrary to the principles of the WTO because they can be used as protectionist instruments? Where do we stand on the US insistence upon outdated phytosanitary rules as part of their protectionist stance? Does Europe have the right and perhaps the duty to take a different view of food, which reflects our history, our culture and our beliefs?

These are the issues that will press ministers in the very near future. Add to them the demands of the animal welfarists; the need to reform the Common Agricultural Policy (CAP); the appalling effect of our subsidies on poor countries; the worldwide collapse of fish stocks; the growing desertification; and the increasing effects of climate change on food production and you will see why I believe that food will preoccupy ministers, here and abroad, for as long ahead as anyone can imagine.

Rt Hon John Gummer MP is a former chairman of the Conservative Party, Minister for Agriculture, Fisheries and Food and Secretary of State for the Environment. Since leaving office, he has been awarded the title 'Parliamentarian who did most for the environment internationally' by the BBC, and he has been appointed chairman of the International Commission on Sustainable Consumption.

Farming today: food science and subsidy

The output and competitiveness of European farming can be increased without endangering the environment, but reform of food policies is essential if fair global food trade is to be achieved

Chris Haskins

The main concern of mankind throughout history has been the supply of food. Two centuries ago, the Reverend Malthus forecast that the world's population would soar and the demand for food would exceed supply. However, thanks to man's ingenuity, whilst the planet's population has risen sixfold since the days of Malthus, there is less danger of widespread famine than ever before.

However, in recent years, there has been growing concern that modern farming methods are endangering the environment, and pressure groups urge that governments should restrain such practices. The great question, therefore, is whether the world can feed a population set to increase by 50 per cent over the next 50 years – from 6 billion to 9 billion – if, at the same time, modern farming techniques, including scientific innovation such as genetic modification, are restricted through regulation.

As always in policy-making, trade-offs are inevitable. Many farm practices, particularly the excessive and reckless use of chemicals and over-intensive livestock production, will have to be reined in; however, if the world had to rely entirely on organic farming methods it would starve within months. The problem for policy-makers is that political clout has passed from the producers, who applied chemicals irresponsibly and without challenge, to the environmentalists, many of whom, rejecting most scientific innovation (including GM development), are behaving equally irresponsibly.

The global nature of these controversies adds further difficulties as countries adopt different positions on these issues. Europe and the US are at odds about GM development, and the British don't care for Spain's approach to animal welfare. In affluent countries, food-related health problems are now predominantly caused by over-eating, while malnutrition caused by food shortages remains the major concern for poorer countries, especially in Africa.

World Trade Organisation (WTO) countries are committed to a significant liberalisation of global trade in food but, here again, there are conflicting stances. The powerful farmers' lobby in the EU and the US wants to maintain protectionist policies that block imports from elsewhere and result in the dumping of surpluses on world markets, with disastrous consequences for the farmers in the developing world. The latter are understandably keen to eliminate these barriers so that they can access the rich countries' markets.

There is a third group – the anti-globalisation alliance of protectionist trade unions and radical Greens – who want to increase, rather than reduce, trade barriers in order to 'protect' domestic industries, including farming.

Food safety and EU membership

Yet another area of potential conflict relates to food safety. The BSE catastrophe has alarmed European consumers and high-lighted serious shortcomings in national food safety regulations. The answer must be to create effective EU safety standards but it is hard to get the member states to agree on an agenda. Many of the new EU member states will have to raise their food safety standards significantly before they become full members.

Perceptions about food safety vary between countries and, especially, between the US and the EU. The US operates tough border controls on food imports, but objects to the EU's concerns about the use of hormones in beef production.

The main conclusion from this analysis is that food policy and regulation are now an EU and international matter. National food strategies were a consequence of wartime shortages, when it was deemed that self-sufficiency in food production was the only answer to the U-boat blockade of supplies from abroad. That threat no longer exists. In signing up to the Treaty of Rome and the Single European Market, all EU members had to abide by the CAP, with all its shortcomings. For obvious reasons, 80 per cent of environmental regulations are derived from EU directives and only 20 per cent from national legislation.

A further increase in EU and international regulation of food and agriculture is inevitable, unless one subscribes to the views of right-wing isolationalists and left-wing anti-globalists. The agenda is formidable.

The world must agree that agri-science is allowed to develop, consistent with a sustainable environment. Crucially, this development must include the use of GM, subject, of course, to extensive testing. Without GM, the poorer, largely subtropical countries may not be able to produce the extra food they need because of the extremes of weather and diseases that ravage their plants and livestock. (Probably the greatest scientific benefit of the past 30 years was the development of straw stiffeners that enabled farmers to grow wheat that would remain standing after severe rainfall. This is why India is now a net exporter of wheat.)

The justification for GM technology lies in its control of disease in plants and animals, resulting in higher yields and the lowering of food production costs through a reduction of the use of chemicals, which in turn should enhance, rather than detract from, a sustainable environment.

It is even harder to apply international standards of food safety because perceptions of risk vary from country to country. In poorer countries, supply is more critical than safety, and the cost of achieving Europe's standards may be prohibitive. But there are also differences in attitude between the rich countries. The less risk averse North Americans accept mortality rates from food that are six times higher than those of Britain; US consumers appear to have little concern about the presence of GM and beef hormones in their food, whereas the impact of BSE and emotional definitions of GM as 'Frankenstein' food have created widespread anxiety amongst European consumers.

Governments must start by establishing minimalist non-negotiable safety standards for trade in food, including basic process requirements and bacteriological standards. Differences over GM and the use of hormones must be resolved and, somehow, the concerns of consumers, especially in Europe, have to be alleviated.

The EU and US, therefore, should sign up to policies which promote a sustainable environment, scientific development and food safety – policies which are global and take proper account of the needs of poorer countries and their ability to comply.

The EU's CAP, for many years, has been heavily criticised in Britain and a small number of other member states with little effect, as the French remained obdurate and the Germans were prepared to write the cheques. But a less confident Germany is no longer willing to be the EU's sugar daddy and, if current policies were applied to the new members in the East, the cost would escalate further.

The CAP, in its present form, will need to be radically reformed if the EU is to meet its WTO commitment to liberalise global trade in food. Those negotiations commence in Doha in the spring of 2003.

In anticipation of these events – enlargement and WTO – the European Commission has proposed some reforms that are a step in the right direction and, although France and the other beneficiaries of the existing policies have shown signs of intransigence, they too must recognise that a fairer deal for Africa necessitates radical reform of European protectionist policies. At last, one feels, there is a real opportunity for change.

Farming is not just an industry

However, it is unrealistic to treat farming in the same way as any other industry. For a start, whilst supplies of food are far less vulnerable to military action, especially in the West, the vagaries of the weather require political intervention to guarantee an adequate supply of safe affordable food. Next, if there were no state support at all, and markets were allowed to prevail, large areas of the countryside would become derelict, to the dismay of tax-paying citizens who appear prepared to pay to maintain a thriving rural society. Finally, consumer and environmental concerns will oblige governments to regulate the food chain more extensively than any other industry. So the question is not about withdrawing state support for agriculture, but applying that support so that it is fairer to smaller, poorer farmers in the world and promotes, rather than undermines, a sustainable environment.

Yet another politically tricky issue is about where the balance of power lies between consumers, retailers, manufacturers and farmers. Consumers point out that producer interest has dominated policy, whereas farmers complain that manufacturers and retailers exercise excessive buying power over them. British farmers grumble about their supermarket customers, and their African neighbours feel exploited by multinational manufacturers. A fair WTO settlement should address the concern of the African farmer and competition rules in Britain and Europe, which nowadays are designed almost exclusively to protect the consumer interest and need to be broadened to ensure that the supermarket buyers do not exploit their power. There are serious regulatory implications in such a change; so, for the moment, codes of good practice and self-regulation should be given a chance before introducing more state regulation.

Finally, there are two crucial areas where individual initiative rather than state intervention is the best way of solving problems: farming competitiveness and diet.

There is enormous scope for improving the output and competitiveness of European farming without endangering the environment. Technological development will result in speedier, more efficient cultivation and harvesting, thereby mitigating the impact of unfavourable weather, increasing the size of farms and reducing the numbers of workers. Migration from the countryside has been taking place in Britain for nearly two centuries but elsewhere this process is only just beginning. People only leave the countryside because work in the towns is more attractive. Today in Britain, farming, in crisis, still suffers from more labour shortages than any other industry – our daffodils, strawberries and cauliflowers would not be harvested without an influx of migrant workers from Eastern Europe.

In addition to all this, there is the growing health crisis arising out of diet. The rise of obesity in Britain in the past 20 years has been startling, such that, if the trend continues, today's children may enjoy a lower life expectation than their parents – a complete reversal of the trends of the last two centuries. The cause of being overweight is that people consume more calories than they can burn off. The transformation of work, from being physically vigorous to being largely sedentary, has dramatically reduced the need for high calorie intake, and our metabolisms have indeed adjusted to this change – sugar consumption has nearly halved in a century. But intake is still much too high, compounded by the increased use of the motorcar and the decline in leisurely exercise.

We can tackle this problem in two ways – adjustments to our diet and adjustments to our life style. Governments can play a part in tackling these issues, particularly the deprivation of poverty, but also in influencing children at school about the way they eat. There also needs to be more research aimed at improving the quality of food; for example, breeding cows that produce less butterfat in milk.

However, the most important response to the problem of diet is to get people to take far more exercise because, as well as being the most effective way of burning up calories, this will also tackle other health problems to do with lungs and circulation. Children should be encouraged to walk to school and to play more physical games. Adults know very well that exercise is good for them. Governments can encourage, but people have to decide for themselves.

Food has always been highly political, but never more so than at present. Reform of food policies is essential if the benefits of EU enlargement and fairer free global trade are to be achieved. A proper balance must be struck between policies aimed at providing a growing world population with an adequate supply of safe, affordable food and regulations needed to maintain the environment. Imaginative policies are essential to tackle the two great health problems relating to food shortage in Africa and over-indulgence in the West. If we could resolve the international problem of food, we would be taking a significant step towards international cooperation on a whole range of other issues.

Chris Haskins is the former chairman of Northern Foods, and has been a member of the Commission on Social Justice, a member of the UK Round Table on Sustainable Development and Chairman of the UK Government's Better Regulation Task Force. He became a life peer in 1998 and was appointed by the Prime Minister to advise on rural recovery in the UK in the aftermath of the outbreak of foot-and-mouth disease in 2001.

Gut reaction: the real risks of food poisoning

Food scares have created the false impression that public health is at greater risk than a century ago, but people are still dying unnecessarily

Hugh Pennington

What happened in 1984? Forget about George Orwell for the moment. On Saturday 25 August, a supper of cold roast beef contaminated with *Salmonella* was served at Stanley Royd Hospital, near Wakefield. During the next two weeks, 355 patients and 106 staff fell ill. Nineteen patients died. In September, the brain of cow 142 from Pitsham Farm, Sussex, was sent for pathological examination. That summer, with some of its sisters, the cow had become nervous and had started to stagger. It was the first case of BSE to be pathologically confirmed. The first cases of *E.coli* O157 infections ever to be diagnosed in Scotland occurred in 1984. And early in the morning of 27 March, potted palms were put in the turbine hall of No. 4 reactor at the VI Lenin Nuclear Power Station, Chernobyl, as part of its ceremonial opening later that day. Before 1984, hardly any journalists and even fewer members of the public had heard of *Salmonella* and *E.coli* O157, let alone Chernobyl. But these bacteria and BSE were to conspire with a public perception already there before Chernobyl, but mightily strengthened when reactor No. 4 blew up at 1.23am on 26

April 1986, to drive food safety to the top of the policy agenda and seriously damage the standing of ministers, officials, the government machine, scientists and science itself. It was their misfortune to be responsible when two powerful forces collided, one a belief held by many that we live in a 'risk society', and the other the working of evolution in real time.

The German sociologist Ulrich Beck championed the 'risk society' paradigm.[1] He claims that the risks of late modernity are new. They are global invisible products of industrialization and overproduction understandable only in scientific terms. Their effects are potentially catastrophic. Beck says that 'the movement set in motion by the risk society . . . is expressed in the statement: "I am afraid!"'. Mary Douglas and Aaron Wildavsky put it nicely: 'What are Americans afraid of? Nothing much, really, except the food they eat, the water they drink, the air they breathe, the land they live on, and the energy they use.'[2] It is easy to understand why belief in the risk society is strong. Our brains are hard-wired for fear, part of the mechanism that has evolved to help us to survive external threats; above a certain threshold it kicks in and primes us to fight or flee. The brains of BSE victims both bovine and human are damaged by the causative agent in a way which causes the fear centre to be turned on inappropriately. Sufferers from vCJD have horrible nightmares and howl uncontrollably. Disgust is another human emotion deeply embedded in our nervous systems. Aversion to faeces and foul smells is rapidly learned when we are very young and is held on to tenaciously. It is only lost with dementia, madness, or death. The development of powerfully effective lobbyists and pressure groups concerned with pollution was aided and driven by these emotions.

Risk, fear and the media
The paradox that belief in the risk society, and the fear that it brings, is strongest in the richest countries (with the healthiest populations enjoying ever increasing life expectancies) testifies to the effectiveness of those pressure groups. But it would be wrong to ascribe the strength of fear only to worries about the levels of damage that pollutants might cause. Concerns are magnified many times when exposure to them is involuntary. People are far more exercised about rail than road safety,

1 Beck, U et al, 1992, *Risk society*, Sage, London, p 49.
2 Douglas, M and Wildavsky, AB, 1982, *Risk and culture*, University of California Press, Berkeley, p 10.

though they know in their heart of hearts that they are far more likely to be killed by their own driving in their own car.

For food safety there is another fear-inducing factor. Food poisoning outbreaks are newsworthy. So it is not surprising that *Salmonella* at Stanley Royd induced a significant political response – a public inquiry. There were many lessons to learn. The inquiry report told a story of unremitting horror; of wards full of doubly incontinent 'difficult' patients with diarrhoea during a heat wave over a Bank Holiday weekend, of hospital kitchens built in 1865 with open drains harbouring eviction-resistant cockroaches and even a rat with *Salmonella* (it had wandered in and was a victim, not the cause) among many more such nightmares. Some good came out of all this. Hospitals lost crown immunity. But *Salmonella* did not go away as a political issue. It struck again through Edwina Currie. In the summer of 1988, there had been a rapid increase of food poisoning caused by a new kind of chicken *Salmonella*. Infected laying hens were not sick, but the bacterium got into their reproductive systems and, on and off, their eggs. Dishes made from pooled raw egg caused human infections. Edwina said on ITN, 'most of the egg production in this country, sadly, is now infected with *Salmonella*.' Egg consumption plummeted. In her own words to the BSE Inquiry:

> both MAFF and the producers took a dim view of my action: they regarded me as the problem, and that if I were removed the issue would go away. I was informed that writs had been served and I resigned from office on 16 December. Subsequently I discovered that there were no writs.

In February, Margaret Thatcher set up a cabinet committee on food safety, MISC 138. By April, a Food Bill was decided upon. It became law the following year. The Act was a good one, one of Thatcher's best deeds. It works well still. But it was not enough to avert a much bigger storm.

Mad cows

Since 1984, BSE had become a common cattle disease, particularly in dairy cows. By the mid-1990s, quite a lot had been learned about it. Infection was spread by meat and bone-meal feed supplements that contained cooked protein from dead animals that had, or were incubating, the disease. Its use had been stopped. Offal that could contain the BSE agent no longer went into the human food chain. The levels of disease in cows peaked in 1993. But whether BSE could infect humans was not known. The government's view was that the possibility was 'remote', a word that came from a committee chaired by Sir Richard Southwood, an eminent Oxford zoologist. Contrary opinions expressed in public by people like Professor Richard Lacey were contradicted. Cautionary private words from officials on the periphery like the Welsh Chief Medical Officer Deirdre Hine met with the response 'mind your own business.' But the policy fell apart at 3.31pm on 20 March 1996 when the Minister of Health, Stephen Dorrell, announced to the House of Commons that ten young people had contracted a new variant of vCJD and that it was probable that they had caught BSE. Sales collapsed. But by far the most important casualty was trust. For almost a decade, the public had been strung along with false reassurances. In the words of the BSE Inquiry Report, members of the public had been subjected to a policy of sedation. They didn't like it. Onora O'Neill[3] opened her 2002 Reith Lectures with Confucius' words telling his disciple Tzu-kung that

> *three things are needed for government: weapons, food and trust. If a ruler can't hold on to all three, he should give up the weapons first and the food next. Trust should be guarded to the end: without trust we cannot stand.*

As a final blow to public confidence in 1996, *E.coli* O157 struck in central Scotland in November and December. In similar circumstances to those found at Stanley Royd Hospital, meat from John Barr and Sons' butchers shop poisoned 500 people and killed 17.

Risky science?

The personal tragedy of the victims must come at the top of the list of the evils wrought by these infections. But there were other bad consequences. Beck's 'risk society' paradigm got a major boost. Food scares and their increasing frequency proved the malignancy

3 O'Neill O, 2002, *A question of trust: BBC Reith Lectures 2002*, Cambridge University Press, Cambridge.

of modernity. The scale of the problem was perceived to be terrifying. Science was to blame and science was out of control.

The difficulty with all this is that Beck's analysis of modern problems is facile and profoundly unhistorical. The risks we run are far less than ever before. To reach adulthood a century ago we had to negotiate infantile gastroenteritis, diphtheria, polio, scarlet fever and measles. Typhoid fever was still busy; smallpox outbreaks occurred regularly. An inadequate diet put our immune systems below par so that osteomyelitis was common and tuberculosis fatal; coupled with gross air pollution shutting out the sun, it gave many of us rickets. To be fair to 'risk society' believers, it would be wrong to give modern developments a clean bill of health. The spread of *Salmonella* in chicken flocks was helped enormously by the concentration of the industry in a few hands and intensive production methods. But to say that BSE was the work of latter-day white-coated Frankensteins would be equally wrong. Its infectious agent evolved through natural processes. It was spread by feeding animals meat and bone meal, a practice developed empirically by farmers a century ago to tide animals over the winter, then coupled by them with traditional breeding practices aimed at increasing milk yields. It is a myth that deregulating the production of meat and bone meal was to blame, by allowing scrapie from sheep to survive and cause BSE. The process was never regulated in the first place; all evidence indicates that scrapie and BSE are not the same.

However, BSE is invoked whenever science-based developments in food are being opposed. Those who are against GM technologies refer to it constantly as an example of the horrors that could follow if GM plants were grown or GM foods consumed. Its rhetorical power is very great, but GM is test-tube science. BSE's origins were very different. The BSE problem was not caused or made worse by a surfeit of science, but by a lack of it. The 1989 'remoteness' conclusion was never ever subjected to expert scientific review until years after BSE had first appeared.

Don't blame science

Salmonella, *E.coli* O157 and BSE teach us three big lessons. First, we are very bad at learning them. The mistakes made in the kitchens at Stanley Royd Hospital in 1984 were repeated in John Barr's butchers business in Wishaw in November 1996.

Second, evolution is constantly throwing up new challenges. *E.coli* O157 and BSE were brand new in the 1980s. Spending money on anticipatory research and surveillance is a sound insurance policy; the 1980s science cutbacks helped BSE. Third, infectious agents will punish us heavily when defences against them are neglected – the strongest defences being those with the strongest scientific foundations.

Set up mainly in response to BSE, the Food Standards Agency started work in April 2000. In British terms, it is setting new standards for openness. But openness will not be enough. In Britain, we have a particular problem in using our best scientists to inform policy; did Sir Richard Southwood's committee consult the world-class scientists working in Edinburgh on transmissible spongiform encephalopathies (diseases like scrapie and BSE) during its deliberations or was the World Reference Laboratory on foot and mouth disease at Pirbright in Surrey asked for its views when contingency plans were being prepared? No.

In *Down and Out in Paris and London*,[4] George Orwell describes life as a *plongeur* in Paris restaurants. He contrasted shining restaurant brass with unspeakably unhygienic kitchens. He would have understood how, in 1996, John Barr could infect 500 people with contaminated meat yet be voted 'Scottish Butcher of the Year' by customers who only saw the front shop. Orwell died of tuberculosis in 1950. Looking back on his disease puts recent problems in perspective. Between 1912 and 1937, 65,000 people in England and Wales died from bovine tuberculosis contracted by drinking contaminated raw milk. That even a quarter as many people will die from *Salmonella*, *E.coli* O157 and BSE combined in the next 25 years is very improbable. But it is likely that some of those that do, will die unnecessarily, like those killed by raw milk, because of the imperfect application of science.

Hugh Pennington is Professor of Bacteriology at the University of Aberdeen. He chaired an inquiry for the government into the 1996 Central Scotland E.coli O157 outbreak. He is a member of the Food Standards Agency Scottish Food Advisory Committee, and is a Fellow of the Royal Society of Edinburgh and the Academy of Medical Sciences.

4. Orwell, G, 1983(1933), *Down and out in Paris and London*, Harvest Books, New York.

Cultivating trust

Confidence in food production must be built up by better labelling and consumer information

Renate Künast

'Trust is a delicate plant; once destroyed, it doesn't grow back quickly.' When Otto von Bismarck made this observation in the late nineteenth century, he probably did not mean to include consumer trust in food safety. At that time, and until well into the second half of the twentieth century, this aspect played, at most, a minor role in food production. The central task of the agri-food sector was to produce sufficient food at the lowest possible price. These times are now over. Most people in industrial countries have secure quantities of food, so consumers increasingly focus on food safety and food quality, including subjective and ethical issues like animal welfare and environmental protection.

The arrival of 'mad cow' disease (BSE), outbreaks of foot-and-mouth disease and various food scandals have deeply shaken consumer confidence in the safety of the food they buy and eat. Such problems have also led consumers to question previous agri-food policies, including the comprehensive payments granted to farmers. The time was ripe for a fundamental re-orientation of farm and food policies, since it was perfectly obvious that the path taken previously would lead to a dead end.

Today's new agri-food policies are geared, first and foremost, to the interests of consumers. Consumer protection, full information about production methods and improved product quality are now the priorities. These new policies encourage sustainable food production and promote consumer choices that support sustainable production methods. The re-orientation of agri-food policies also means becoming more market-oriented in our approach. This means phasing out production subsidies and helping farmers to hold their own in competitive markets by improved quality and additional services, like farm-based leisure activities. This way, farmers can achieve added value and income in secure rural jobs.

But food safety must be the overriding imperative. There cannot be any compromise in this area, since safeguarding health takes priority over economic interests. Placing safe food on the market must simply be a matter of course. All operators in the food chain, from farmers to retailers via distributors, are responsible for food safety. Policymakers, meanwhile, are responsible for providing the legal provisions and efficient controls people need. The consumer is prepared to reward their efforts, as has been seen in the beef industry, where demand for beef, which had fallen sharply, has recovered thanks to rigorous BSE controls.

The question of how food is produced, handled and processed is gaining importance. Ultimately, it is the consumers who determine the desired quality of food and how much they are willing to pay for it. However, in order to make such a choice, consumers must also be able to assess the safety and quality of the foods on offer. This is where policymakers come in: to establish the legal framework and information requirements that will enable consumers to make informed decisions. Only then will consumers feel more confident in selecting or rejecting certain products and will the market reward better quality.

Uniform labelling

Comprehensive food labelling is particularly important. Uniform labels help consumers to discern quality. In Germany, the eco-labelling system offers a simple, uniform way for consumers to distinguish organic products from other foods quickly and easily, to the benefit of consumers, retailers, farmers and the processing industry. Products from developing countries or other EU member states can also qualify for the German eco-label as long as they comply with the EU standard on which the label is based.

Our model is sustainable agriculture and food production. The social costs of 'ever more at ever lower prices' must be reduced. Natural resources must be preserved for both current and future generations. As organic farming is already clearly geared to sustainability, support for organic farming and for sales of organic produce is an essential building block in re-orienting agri-food policies. Germany aims to increase the organic sector's share to 20 per cent of the land being farmed within ten years.

Yet this is not all there is to re-orienting agri-food policies. The goal is to gear farming to sustainability by supporting environmentally benign and welfare-friendly production methods. In the past few months, many measures have been adopted to this effect in Germany, ensuring that public money for farming is targeted to sustainable methods such as improving animal welfare or preserving biodiversity. An additional priority is to strengthen rural areas as business locations. We must not forget that economic efficiency and the competitiveness of enterprises are the basic prerequisites for achieving this.

But a new direction is needed beyond national level if we are to attain our objectives. European agricultural policy must take the social demands on agriculture fully into account. For this reason, it is in our interest to use the forthcoming mid-term review of Agenda 2000 to initiate a fundamental re-orientation of EU agricultural policy. The cornerstones of our reform policies at European level were laid out in Agenda 2000, covering the period 2000–6. The key elements are reinforced market orientation and quality competition, reduction of production support instruments and more support for rural development. There are a number of other reasons for re-orienting agricultural policy, such as EU enlargement (more farmers in the Union) and the World Trade Organisation (WTO) negotiations on agriculture; not forgetting implementation of the Agenda 21 agreements on sustainable development adopted by the Earth Summit in Rio de Janeiro in 1992 and no doubt up for discussion at the World Summit on Sustainable Development in Johannesburg.

As well as producing safe food, agriculture renders many important social services. Changing demands from society open up opportunities for developing new sources of income. Instead of indiscriminately handing out subsidies more or less evenly based on the amount produced, socially desired services of agriculture, such as keeping the land viable for future generations, providing a habitat for rare wild animals and plants, or providing tourist activities, must be rewarded in a targeted way. This is all the more true if they cannot be remunerated through the market or if they are linked to requirements the farmers have to meet, such as reducing pesticide use. This is also the only way to convince the consumer that supporting agriculture is in the interests of society.

This way, the circle starting and ending with the consumer is complete. Good agri-food policies can help strengthen Bismarck's delicate plant of trust mentioned at the start and return to agriculture the social credit it deserves. 'Trust through change' must be our motto.

Renate Künast is the Federal Minister for Consumer Protection, Food and Agriculture in Germany. 'Rethinking agriculture and food', written by Renate Künast, was first published in the OECD Observer *No. 233 in August 2002. Copyright © OECD (http://www.oecdobserver.org).*

'Big Food': politics and nutrition in the United States

The complicity of the food industry and democratically elected politicians in the US is undermining people's health

Marion Nestle

The food industry has given us a food supply so plentiful, so varied, so inexpensive, and so devoid of dependence on geography or season that all but the very poorest of Americans can obtain enough energy and nutrients to meet biological needs. The overly abundant food supply, combined with a society so affluent that most people can afford to buy more food than they need, sets the stage for competition. The food industry must compete fiercely for every dollar spent on food, and food companies expend extraordinary resources to develop and market products that will sell, regardless of their effect on nutritional status or waistlines. To satisfy shareholders, food companies must convince people to *eat more* of their products or to eat their products instead of those of competitors. They do so through advertising and public relations, of course, but also by working tirelessly to convince government officials, nutrition professionals, and the media that their products promote health – or at least do no harm. Much of this work is a virtually invisible part of contemporary culture that attracts only occasional notice.

Nutrition scientists and practitioners typically believe that food companies are genuinely interested in improving health. They think it makes sense to work with the industry to help people improve their diets, and most are outraged by suggestions that food industry sponsorship of research or programs might influence what they do or say. Most food company officials maintain that any food product can be included in a balanced, varied, and moderate diet; they say that their companies are helping to promote good health when they fund the activities of nutrition professionals.

In this political system, the actions of food companies are normal. The primary mission of food companies, like that of tobacco companies, is to sell products. Food companies are not health or social service agencies, and nutrition becomes a factor in corporate thinking only when it can help sell food. The ethical choices involved in such thinking are considered all too rarely.

Humans do not innately know how to select a nutritious diet; we survived in evolution because nutritious foods were readily available for us to hunt or gather. In an economy of overabundance, food companies can sell products only to people who want to buy them. Whether consumer demands drive food sales or the industry creates such demands is a matter of debate, but much industry effort goes into trying to figure out what the public 'wants' and how to meet such 'needs'. Nearly all research on this issue yields the same conclusion. When food is plentiful and people can afford to buy it, basic biological needs become less compelling and the principal determinant of food choice is personal preference. In turn, personal preferences may be influenced by religion and other cultural factors, as well as by considerations of convenience, price and nutritional value. To sell food in an economy of abundant food choices, companies must worry about those other determinants much more than about the nutritional value of their products – unless the nutrient content helps to entice buyers. Thus the food industry's marketing imperatives principally concern four factors: taste, cost, convenience, and public confusion.

- *Taste: make foods sweet, fatty, and salty*
  Adults prefer foods that taste, look, and smell good, are familiar and provide variety, but these preferences are influenced strongly by family and ethnic background, level of education, income, age, and gender. When asked, most of us prefer sweet foods and those that are 'energy-dense' (high in calories, fat, and sugar), and we like the taste of salt. Such preferences drive the development of new food products as well as the menus in restaurants.

- *Cost: add value but keep prices low*
  One result of overabundance is pressure to add value to foods through processing. The producers of raw foods receive only a fraction of the price that consumers pay at the supermarket. In 1998, for example, an average of 20 per cent of retail cost – the 'farm value' of the food – was returned to its producers. The remaining 80 per cent of the food dollar goes for labor, packaging, advertising, and other such value-enhancing activities. Conversion of potatoes (cheap) to potato chips (expensive) to those fried in artificial fats or coated in soybean flour or herbal supplements (even more expensive) is an example of how value is added to basic food commodities.

- *Convenience: make eating fast*
  Convenience is a principal factor driving the development of value-added products. The demographic causes of demands for convenience are well understood. In the last quarter of the twentieth century, the proportion of women with children who entered the workforce greatly expanded, and many people began to work longer hours to make ends meet. Many of these products are high in calories, fat, sugar, or salt but are marketed as nutritious because they contain added vitamins.

  Nutritionists and traditionalists may lament such developments, because convenience overrides not only considerations of health but also the social and cultural meanings of meals and mealtimes. In the meantime, convenience adds value to foods and stimulates the food industry to create even more products that can be consumed quickly and with minimal preparation.

- *Confusion: keep the public puzzled*
Many people find it difficult to put nutrition advice into practice, not least because they view the advice as ephemeral – changing from one day to the next. This view is particularly unfortunate because advice to eat more fruits and vegetables and to avoid overweight as a means to promote health has remained constant for half a century (see Figure 1). Confusion about nutrition is quite understandable, however. People obtain information about diet and health from the media – newspapers, magazines, television, radio and, more recently, the internet.

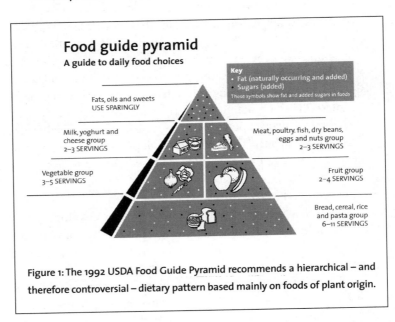

Food guide pyramid
A guide to daily food choices

Key
- Fat (naturally occurring and added)
- Sugars (added)
These symbols show fat and added sugars in foods

Fats, oils and sweets
USE SPARINGLY

Milk, yoghurt and cheese group
2–3 SERVINGS

Meat, poultry, fish, dry beans, eggs and nuts group
2–3 SERVINGS

Vegetable group
3–5 SERVINGS

Fruit group
2–4 SERVINGS

Bread, cereal, rice and pasta group
6–11 SERVINGS

Figure 1: The 1992 USDA Food Guide Pyramid recommends a hierarchical – and therefore controversial – dietary pattern based mainly on foods of plant origin.

It is in the interest of food companies to have people believe that there is no such thing as a 'good' food (except when it is theirs); that there is no such thing as a 'bad' food (especially not theirs); that all foods (especially theirs) can be incorporated into healthy diets; and that balance, variety, and moderation are the keys to healthy diets – which means that no advice to restrict intake of their particular product is appropriate.

These four imperatives illustrate clearly the limitations of market pressures in developing healthy societies. They lead representatives of food companies and their trade associations to make the following claims:

- The keys to healthy diets are balance, variety, and moderation (especially when their products are included).
- All foods can be part of healthy diets (especially theirs).
- There is no such thing as a good or a bad food (except when their products are considered good).
- Dietary advice changes so often that we need not follow it (unless it favors their products).
- Research on diet and health is so uncertain that it is meaningless (except when it supports the health benefits of their products).
- Only a small percentage of the population would benefit from following population-based dietary advice (if that advice suggests restrictions on intake of their products).
- Diets are a matter of personal responsibility and freedom of choice (especially the freedom to choose their products).
- Advocacy for more healthy food choices is irrational (if it suggests eating less of their products).
- Government intervention in dietary choice is unnecessary, undesirable and incompatible with democratic institutions (unless it protects and promotes their products).

The environment of food choice

Most of us, if we choose to do so, can recognize how food companies spend money on advertising, but it is far more difficult to know about the industry's behind-the-scenes efforts in Congress, federal agencies, courts, universities, and professional organizations to make diets seem a matter of personal choice rather than of deliberate manipulation. The emphasis on individual choice serves the interests of the food industry for one critical reason: if diet is a matter of individual free will, then the only appropriate remedy for poor diets is education, and nutritionists should be off teaching people to take personal responsibility for their own diet and health – not how to institute changes to whole systems that might make it easier for everyone to do so.

That suggestions to change the social environment of food

choice are threatening to industry is evident from the vehemence with which trade associations and the business press attack advice to restrict intake of one or another food group, to get 'junk' food out of schools, to label foods more explicitly, or to tax sales of foods to generate funds for nutrition education. Business commentators equate such approaches with nothing less than fascism: 'If [President] Bill Clinton really wants ideas for a healthy eating crusade, he must surely look to the only political regime that thoroughly made them part of national policy: Nazi Germany.'[1]

Cigarette companies famously argue that smoking is a matter of individual choice and that it is wrong for government to interfere unduly in the private lives of citizens. They use science to sow confusion about the harm that cigarettes can cause. They set the standard in use of public relations, advertising, philanthropy, experts, political funding, alliances, lobbying, intimidation, and lawsuits to protect their sales. In efforts to expand markets, they promote cigarette smoking to children and adolescents; to minorities, women, and the poor; and to people in countries throughout the world, developing as well as industrialized. The similarities between the actions of cigarette companies and those of food companies are no coincidence. Some cigarette companies own food companies.

The parallel practices of food companies, however, have elicited nowhere near this level of protest. The principal reasons for this difference must surely lie in the complexity of the messages about foods and their health effects. Unlike the straightforward 'don't smoke' advice, the dietary message can never be 'don't eat.' Instead, it has to be the more complicated and ambiguous 'eat this instead of that,' 'eat this more often than that,' and the overall prescription, 'eat less.'

Ethical or not, a message to eat less meat, dairy, and processed foods is not going to be popular among the producers of such foods. It will have only limited popularity with producers of fruits and vegetables because their scale of production is limited and they cannot easily add value to their products. The message will not be popular with cattle ranchers, meat packers, dairy producers, or milk bottlers; oil seed growers, processors, or transporters; grain producers (most grain is used to feed cattle);

1 Anderson D, 2000, 'Americans get fatter, but refuse to die. How naughty', Wall Street Journal 8 June: A24.

makers of soft drinks, candy bars, and snack foods; owners of fast-food outlets and franchise restaurants; media corporations and advertising agencies; manufacturers and marketers of television sets and computers (where advertising takes place); and, eventually, drug and health care industries likely to lose business if people stay healthier longer.

The range of economic sectors that would be affected if people changed their diets, avoided obesity, and prevented chronic diseases surely rivals the range of industries that would be affected if people stopped smoking cigarettes. Perhaps for this reason, US Department of Agriculture officials believe that really encouraging people to follow dietary guidelines would be so expensive and disruptive to the agricultural economy as to create impossible political barriers. Rather than accepting the challenge and organizing a concerted national campaign to encourage more healthy eating patterns, they propose a more politically expedient solution: the industry should work to improve the food supply through nutrient fortification and the development of functional foods with added nutritional value. Such proposals raise ethical dilemmas of their own. These foods are not necessarily 'healthier', and they encourage people to eat more, not less.

Eat less?

In all too many instances, as we have seen, the government serves business interests at the expense of public health. Achieving a more equitable balance necessarily starts with representative bodies and, therefore, with the reform of laws governing campaign contributions and lobbying. Diet is thus a political issue. Because dietary advice affects food sales, and because companies demand a favorable regulatory environment for their products, dietary practices raise political issues that cut right to the heart of democratic institutions.

Despite demonstrations that advertising can be extraordinarily effective in promoting desirable dietary changes (such as a switch from whole to lower-fat milk), and at a cost of less than one dollar for every person reached, no government agency can possibly spend that kind of money to reach everyone in the population without a substantial change in tax allocations. As incomes rise further, however, health and wellbeing goals become more important. This last observation suggests that a burgeoning economy creates a stronger base of advocacy for dietary change.

Adopting such actions is one way to apply ethical principles, but the higher cost and inconvenience of doing so are certain to preclude those choices for many (if not most) people. Unless we are willing to pay more for food, relinquish out-of-season produce, and rarely buy anything that comes in a package or is advertised on television, we support the current food system every time we eat a meal. That is why voting with our forks must extend beyond the food choices of individuals to larger political arenas. Countless community, state, and national organizations deal with food issues, and it is not difficult to find one to suit any political viewpoint or taste. As has been demonstrated by the support for creating federal standards for organic food, such groups can join together quickly and effectively when an issue of mutual interest emerges. This ability to exercise democratic power holds much hope for achieving a more equitable balance of interests in matters pertaining to food and health.

Marion Nestle is Professor and Chair of the Department of Nutrition and Food Studies at New York University. She has served as a nutrition policy advisor to the US Department of Health and Human Services and as a member of nutrition and science advisory committees to the Department of Agriculture and the Food and Drug Administration. Her book Safe Food: Bacteria, Biotechnology, and Bioterrorism *will be published in March 2003. This is an extract taken from* Food Politics: How the Food Industry Influences Nutrition and Health, *University of California Press, London, 2002.*

Part 3

Well-being and social outcomes

Barbecue of the vanities: nutritional advice since the Renaissance

We are by no means living through the first age of dieting fads and conflicting advice about what we should eat

Steven Shapin

I have an epidemiologist friend who maintains – if I understand him correctly – that you basically play with the cards dealt you by your genes and in utero development, so you might as well eat whatever you like. Dietary expertise is now inevitably a guest at the dinner table, invited or not. It seems to speak with many voices these days, and I can't usually be bothered to sort out real from so-called junk science, even if I could. Like most people of my condition, I encounter expertise in different ways: sometimes friends tell me what the latest scoop is; sometimes I read about it in the papers; sometimes I hear about it from official pronouncements, governmental and professional; sometimes – and this tends to work on me – I encounter expertise face-to-face in a doctor's surgery when I'm feeling more vulnerable than usual.

Neither the cacophony of expertise nor the incoherence of lay responses is new. The first European dietary books began appearing in the late fifteenth century. They were relatively respectful of existing patterns of consumption: not surprisingly, as they tended to be written for a courtly readership by deferential court physicians. It was well understood that the business of government involved banquets and drinking, and that a prince who was fussy about what he would or would not eat could scarcely do a prince's business. As James I instructed his son, 'your dyet should bee accommodatte to your affaires, & not your affaires to your diet.' The job of the dietary writer was, therefore, to work within these conventions, fine tuning them to ensure that courtiers, and those who aspired to that condition, could take into account empirical medical findings about what tended to be good or bad for individuals of different constitutions. So Giovanni Michele Savonarola – the grandfather of the Florentine killjoy – counselled the rulers of Ferrara that 'Hare is not a meat for Lords,' that 'Fava beans are a food for peasants,' and that, while beef was a food fitted for artisans with robust stomachs and coarse constitutions, the prince might eat it if 'corrected' by the right condiments.

In general, however, the advice was *quod sapit nutrit* (if it tastes good, it's probably good for you) and readers were understood instinctively and by habit to do right by their stomachs: 'every man in his humour'; 'you should eat what you are'; *chacun à son goût*. Galenic medical theory offered expert explanations of the counsels of proverbial common sense and custom. It was best to eat what was constitutionally similar to you, and when the balance of qualities in your food (warm, cold, dry and moist) matched those of your own temperament (sanguinary, choleric, phlegmatic or melancholic), then you rightly and naturally relished it.

By the 1530s, expert dietary advice had become more aggressive and less complaisant to courtly custom and genteel convention. The audience for these sorts of book had expanded and changed, and they were increasingly geared to the concerns and lifestyles of the scholarly classes whose sequestered *vita contemplativa* could accommodate a more embracing care of the bodily self and whose self-presentation traditionally worked in elements of secular hypochondria or sacred asceticism. The tone became more hectoring; blanket prohibitions took the place of qualified advice; custom was generally subsumed into the category of 'popular error'; and what pleased your palate was no longer taken as a reliable guide to what secured your health and long life. Courtly extravagance and gourmandise now stood condemned, as it were from the outside: not just because they were morally bad, but because they were bad for you. By the time of Dr Savonarola's more famous grandson, the physicians were throwing dietary delicacies onto bonfires already well stoked with the moral and literary vanities. The dietary advice of the time can be separated into three sections. Albala tries neatly to periodise. In the first period, from the late fifteenth to early sixteenth century, the doctors' presumption was that you were basically healthy, occasionally needing medical expertise to maintain you in that state of health; however, by the second period, stretching from the mid to late sixteenth century, the experts were trying to convince their readers that they were basically ill, requiring constant dietetic monitoring to prevent sickness from becoming disabling or even fatal.

The curse of abundance

The state had a legitimate concern with the health and longevity of its rulers, and medical expertise offered an idiom in which the court could be simultaneously lectured on its moral as well as physiological duties. Banquets were bad for you, and, in general, the consumption at one meal of that variety of foods so loved by courtly gourmands was a recipe for medical disaster. The ancients ate a simple and frugal diet, and it was well attested that they lived hundreds of years. Even now, it was said, their spare diet was the reason peasants lived longer and more healthily than those cursed with wealth and abundance. By the late sixteenth century, medical expertise tended towards consensus on one point: good health and longevity were to be secured by eating simply and eating less, though few went so far as the Venetian gentleman, Luigi Cornaro, his countryman, the mechanical physician Santorio Santorio, or the Flemish Jesuit, Leonard Lessius, in specifying the precise quantity of aliment requisite to maintain the human frame. Cornaro annoyingly lived to 100 years of age on just 12 ounces of food a day, continually producing new 'I-told-you-so' editions of his *Della vita sobria* as he bloomed with geriatric good health, becoming one of the world's first heroes of secular abstinence.

If there was expert agreement on the general virtue of temperance, consensus ended there. Some writers commended fish while many others warned that it was a phlegmatic food, tending towards corruption. Advocating vegetarianism was rare, but writers battled over whether meat eating was actually good for you, and, if so, what meats best promoted health. Some followed St Paul in approving a little wine 'for thy stomach's sake', as an aid to digestion and for the making of good blood; others condemned it because it slowed digestion, drying and toughening food in the stomach. Many writers regarded fresh fruit, particularly peaches, cucumbers and melons, as so viscous and difficult to concoct that they were practically lethal – both Albert II of Bohemia and Pope Paul II were struck down by eating melons – while Girolamo Cardano's *De usu ciborum* identified the 'abstersive', or scouring, virtues of melons, and Prosper Calano reckoned that melons might be safely taken when corrected with a little 'plaisantin cheese', a forerunner of the modern Parmesan.

During the third period, from the late sixteenth to mid seventeenth century, dietary writers became more eclectic and empirical, throwing off the shackles of ancient authority and learning from experience. Prohibitions against melons, for example, were harder to sustain as more people ate them – even 'uncorrected' by parmigiano reggiano – and did not immediately fall down dead. But the tone of expertise was as bullying as ever and, far from presuming that what tasted good was good for you, the experts now increasingly tried to convince you that you could secure health only through a continual battle against appetite. Since the body was in constant need of correction, the food that was best for you was probably the stuff that gave least pleasure. Puritanism was finding a powerful ally among the physicians. Yet, by the later part of the seventeenth century, it seemed that dietary advice would gradually become defunct, a victim of 'the scientific method'. True, newly fashionable Newtonian and Cartesian micro-mechanical theories began the very slow process of squeezing out the old language of virtues, humours, complexions and temperaments but, into the eighteenth century and far beyond, physicians' dietary counsel often remained as bizarre, confident and, above all, heterogeneous as it had ever been.

Continuity and change

In the Renaissance and the early modern period, expertise spoke with so many voices that it is impossible to assess whether or not it had any effect on lay practice. Certainly, by the 1580s, Montaigne had had enough. He'd read the dietary books, and that was the problem; he'd read practically all of them, books by the pro-fish experts and the anti-fish experts: 'If your Physitian thinke it not good that you sleepe, that you drinke wine, or eate such and such meates: Care not you for that; I will finde you another that shall not be of his opinion.' His sentiments are familiar to the modern consumer. Much has changed since the Renaissance in the provision and institutional location of dietary expertise. Dietetics has become a major state concern. Nutritional advice now often speaks with the authority of the state and frequently with the force of law. Some things, however, have remained constant: despite the many scientific advances since the Renaissance, dietetic opinion is often still contradictory.

In the sixteenth century, civic culture had a way of talking back to the experts who advised on how to live long and healthily, a counter which is almost inaudible in late modern culture. Montaigne, for example, doubted that there was genuine expertise to be had, other than that you obtained from your own experience: 'The Arts that promise to keepe our body and minde in good health, promise much unto us; but therewith there is none performeth lesse what they promise.' But even if you could be sure of such expertise, Montaigne thought it was servile to bind yourself rigidly to dietary rules. To make a religion of temperance is unsociable and unbecoming. Occasional surfeit was a condition of sociability, and a refusal to eat what your host put in front of you was incivility. If, in the quest for health and longevity, you made a fetish of abstinence, you might secure your object, but only at the cost of making life not worth living. And if these ascetic physicians 'doe no other good, at least they doe this, that they prepare their patients early for death, undermining little by little and cutting off their enjoyment of life.' The relative absence of these sentiments from contemporary culture testifies to the real respect in which all sorts of medical expertise are held. But the inaudibility of Montaigne's sceptical voice is also a useful index to the decline of the social virtues.

Certain strands of modern expertise have surely made a tactical mistake in abandoning the language in which common sense and prudence have been embedded for millennia: balance, variety and moderation; have a little bit of everything; the occasional indiscretion isn't going to kill you, but don't make a habit of it. The proverbial voice says, 'You are what you eat,' or, more resonantly in German, 'Man ist was er isst.' Modern nutritionists construe that dictum almost solely in molecular terms – if you eat too much animal fat it will clog up your arteries – but the relationship between eating and identity is moral as well as molecular. People eat what, when, how, how much and with whom they do so for a thousand reasons apart from the desire to assuage hunger and to secure a healthy long life: to show love and power; to express amiability or contempt; to display willingness or unwillingness to be part of their society; to demonstrate sophisticated worldliness or insouciant disregard of self; to honour the gods (household, racial, national and celestial); to maintain and make claims to all sorts of social identity; to have something that tastes good.

Steven Shapin teaches sociology at the University of California, San Diego. His books include A Social History of Truth: Civility and Science in Seventeenth-Century England *(University of Chicago Press, 1995). He has written numerous papers on the history and sociology of science. A version of this article originally appeared as part of a review essay of Ken Albala's book* Eating Right in the Renaissance *and Marion Nestle's book* Food Politics *in the* London Review of Books *24(16).*

Working on the food chain gang

Government agencies and other public sector caterers should lead by example by feeding their customers wholesome food

Jeanette Longfield

The farming and food system is often referred to as a food chain. In reality, it's much more like a complex web of interactions, many of them pulling in opposite directions. But another chain analogy is more accurate – the chain gang of the old American penal system, immortalised in movies and popular music. In mythology, the chain gang, dressed in striped pyjamas, broke rocks in the hot sun – punishing work in punishing conditions. In the food chain, the average UK farmer earned just £5,200 in the financial year up to 2001 while gang masters continue to exploit migrant farm workers throughout the EU and, in southern countries, thousands suffer (and sometimes die) from applying the agri-chemicals so integral to industrialised agriculture.

And the product of their respective labours? High volume, low grade raw materials. In one case, rocks; in the other, tonnes of agricultural commodities to be haggled over on the trading floors and transported across the globe. Even for those not working in the food chain gang, the result is alienation from one of our most fundamental sources of pleasure and of life itself. Only around 2 per cent of employment is in UK agriculture. The rest of us would have to search back generations to find a link to the land.

And our food – like us – is on the move. In the decade from 1989, road freight of food and drinks increased by 90 per cent and travelled 51 per cent further. In the decade from 1985, average shopping distances increased by 57 per cent (from 14 to 22 kms) and frequency from 1.7 to 2.4 times per week. A sample of fruit and vegetables from an average supermarket can include Spanish celery, Californian baby spinach and South African baby carrots. It's official: the seasons are abolished and distance is no object.

The agri-food industry will tell you that this is what the consumer wants. In truth, it may be what the consumer *buys*, but that's not the same thing. Do we really want our food supplies to be almost entirely dependent on fossil fuel? The fuel crisis showed how dangerously vulnerable we are even to temporary disruption, but the longer-term trends are more disturbing still. Two-thirds of oil reserves lie in the Middle East. Since the first oil crisis of 1973, the price of oil has doubled or trebled overnight on three occasions. It doesn't take a foreign affairs expert to work out the likelihood of more such jolts to the system. And the oil is running out. Estimates vary and China is a critical factor, since we cannot know how fast that country will accelerate towards European or American levels of over-consumption, but we may have as much as 50 years' worth left, or as few as 20. Even if the calculations are wrong, 100 years of oil supplies wouldn't help much, since the consequences of using them can be as catastrophic as running dry. The reality of climate change caused by burning fossil fuels is now almost universally accepted; however, despite this extraordinary scientific and political consensus leading to fairly hefty, and entirely justifiable, taxation at the petrol pumps, aviation fuel is untaxed. So where you paid 80p for a litre of petrol in November 2000, airlines paid 18p.

Real cost of consumption

Then there are the other energy and environmental costs of food miles. Agri-chemicals, packaging, preservation and storage all need to be accounted for, along with waste disposal. Most of the 80 million food and drinks cans we use every day are not recycled but buried in increasingly scarce landfill sites. We use 12 billion plastic carrier bags every year (an average of 323 per household). Despite the potential to compost or recycle around 70 per cent of household waste, the UK's current recycling rate is a pathetic 9 per cent.

It gets worse. In 1998, 12.3 million pigs, cattle and sheep were traded live within the EU. Despite animal welfare regulations, many animals died en route while others suffered miserable conditions, arriving at their destinations in a pitiful state. Not only does this offend all humane principles but also the trade in animals and meat products increases the risk of spreading disease. While the foot-and-mouth disease disaster was hideous enough, at least the disease is not transmissible to humans. We may not be so lucky with the next outbreak of an animal disease.

And for what? Supermarket shelves appear stuffed with variety, but the packaging conceals the same fatty, sugary and salty mixtures, disguised with colours, flavourings and thickeners to appear different from one another. More than 700 breeds of farm animals have become extinct, and of the hundreds of native varieties of apple, only a handful of different types (not all of them British) will be in a superstore near you. The real story of the food industry to date is not about diversity but homogeneity and standardisation.

The apple, in fact, is a potent symbol, not only of what's wrong with our farming and food system, but also of the fight to put it right. When Common Ground first started Apple Day in the early 1990s they could scarcely have dreamt that, not only would the annual autumn celebrations still be going strong, but that they would also have expanded and spawned glorious imitations. HDRA, the Organic Organisation, now honours the humble spud each year; British cheese, real ale and strawberries all have their own festivals; and October now marks a month-long celebration of British gastronomy.

Organic food, of course, has experienced exponential growth and also uses the traditional harvest festival period to praise the virtues of an holistic approach to the health of the land, animals and people. Farm shops are enjoying a revival, along with the fashionable farmers' markets; there are waiting lists again for allotments, and supermarkets are competing with Michelin-starred restaurants to trumpet the uniqueness of their local specialities. At last the local food Cinderella gets to go to the ball.

Public sector food

The ugly sister in this story is public sector catering. The catering sector as a whole now accounts for around a third of British spending on food, and the proportion is still growing. The public sector is around 7 per cent of this market, with approximately 61,500 outlets and 1.8 billion meals eaten every year in schools, care homes, hospitals, prisons, the armed forces, and government departments and agencies, and the majority of these organisations cater for people with special dietary needs. Children's brains, nervous systems and reproductive organs are still developing. People in nursing homes and hospitals have weakened immune systems and Bernard Gesch argues powerfully, in this volume, for the nutritional vulnerability of some young offenders. Even strapping squaddies, it could be argued, have a particular need for high-quality, nutritious food. But those who need the best appear to get the worst.

Years of spending cuts, the legacy of compulsory competitive tendering, and general denigration of public services have left most institutional food services with derisory budgets and hence the cheapest and nastiest parts of the food system. Most public sector catering does not even have to comply with basic nutritional standards (they have only just been reintroduced to schools and no-one has yet dared to look to see whether standards have improved across the board). Only bare minimums apply in terms of residues of pesticides and veterinary drugs. So, for example, the majority of the free fruit handed out to 4- to 6-year-olds in the Lottery funded government scheme had detectable residues. And it's more than likely that meat containing residues of antibiotics has been dished out to hospital patients. While over-prescribing antibiotics has undoubtedly contributed to the crisis in antibiotic resistance in human medicine, routine use of these drugs on farm animals can't be helping.

A major service to vulnerable groups, funded by significant amounts of tax-payers' money, should surely be supporting the main planks of government policy; reducing health inequalities, promoting sustainable development and regenerating local economies? Whatever happened to 'joined-up government'?

Beating food bureaucracy

When pressed on this point, government is prone to wring its hands and look in mock despair to international and European laws that prevent them pursuing their own policies. It is true that competition laws cooked up by the World Trade Organisation (WTO) and European Union (EU) appear, on the face of it, to prevent governments discriminating in favour of local producers when issuing contracts. Local government rules also seem to present similar obstacles but it doesn't help that domestic supplies of some products can't meet existing, let alone increased demand. Around 70 per cent of organic food bought in the UK is imported and, although the government is now committed to increasing the proportion of domestically supplied organic food, following successful pressure by the Organic Targets Campaign coalition, meeting the targets will take time. Even conventional suppliers are struggling; around half of our vegetables are imported, as is a whopping 90 per cent of our fruit.

Just to complete the obstacle course, many local growers and food businesses are too small to supply the volumes necessary for some public sector outlets. This means either buyers have to stitch together a patchwork of small firms (which is time and labour intensive, neither of which are abundant in the public sector), or suppliers need to collaborate with each other to make life easier for buyers, but may risk the wrath of the Competition Commission.

Insurmountable as these barriers may seem, they are not. Schools, hospitals, nurseries and canteens – in Britain and worldwide – have found imaginative ways around, over and under them. Sustain is working with its member organisations on a Sustainable Food Chains project which, among other things, aims to celebrate and promote these successes, set up some pilot projects to show what more can be done, and produce a toolkit for sustainable public sector catering.

In Cornwall, for example, the County Council's in-house service provider is backing local food suppliers as part of a £1 million contract to supply school meals to 32 primary and secondary schools. So far, around £350,000 worth of contracts have been awarded – all within EU and local authority rules – to four local suppliers for fresh meat, groceries and provisions, frozen foods and vegetables.

The Sustainable Development Commission has asked Liverpool University to investigate the potential for the NHS to use its considerable food purchasing power to support sustainable development. Work by London's King's Fund has already suggested that public health can be improved in deprived areas by using NHS purchasing contracts to support local employment.

Even more promising is the Public Procurement Working Group, established by the Department for Environment, Food and Rural Affairs to look at central government purchasing. While its remit extends to all goods and services, not just food, recommendations (due before the end of 2002) will be made not only to DEFRA's Secretary of State, but also to the Chief Secretary to the Cabinet and the Deputy Prime Minister.

Arguably the best examples of what can be achieved with an appreciation of good food, a willingness to pay and appropriate legislation are to be found abroad. Austria, Denmark, France, Japan, Sweden and the USA all have inspirational examples of public sector catering that creates decent jobs, respects environmental and nutritional principles, and tastes fantastic, but Italy is 'market leader' in good practice. Italian laws date back to 1986 and now oblige local authorities to include organic and quality local products in school menus. There are over 300 examples of organic school meals services, mainly in the north and centre of the country but now spreading south and to the Italian islands. Two years ago, Ferrara (population 133,000) explored the feasibility of including organic and traditional food in school meals without prohibitive increases in costs. These days, around half the ingredients are organic (rising to 80% in nurseries) and the average price of a meal has risen by around 13 per cent.

That, surely, is a small price to pay to escape the chain gang?

Jeanette Longfield is Co-ordinator of Sustain: the alliance for better food and farming (www.sustainweb.org). This article is based on work by Vicki Hird, Andy Jones and James Petts.

Getting better: food in the NHS

Hospital catering should link medical care
to healthy eating

Loyd Grossman

I have to apologize for beginning with The Great Cliché: 'You are
what you eat.' Or more accurately, as written by Brillat-Savarin in
the early nineteenth century, 'Tell me what you eat: I will tell you
what you are.' His dictum was part of a long line of pre-genetic
explanations of how climate, topography and inevitably food
shaped human character and wellbeing. More than 2000 years
earlier, Herodotus looked at the most traumatic event of his
lifetime – the dynamic expansion of the Persian Empire and its
threat to the Greek way of life – and wanted to understand why
the Persians were so different from other peoples. His invented
dialogue for the Persian king explained that 'Soft countries breed
soft men. . . . It is not the property of any one soil to produce fine
fruits and good soldiers too.' Not long afterwards, Hippocrates
began to forge the explicit link between food and health. 'Food is
medicine – hence let your medicine be your food.' Hippocrates
also observed: 'the Art of Medicine would not have been invented
if when men are indisposed the same food . . . which they eat
when in good health were proper for them.' So the intense relationship between what we eat and how we feel is thousands of
years old and by no means exclusive to the Western tradition. In

the Bhagavad Gita, Krishna tells us that 'Men who are pure like food which is pure, which gives health, mental strength and long life; which has taste, is soothing and nourishing and which makes glad the heart of man.'

Given this long and almost universal belief that food plays a major part in our health and healing, it seems surprising that in so may countries today hospital catering isn't at the front line of clinical care. The obvious explanation is that the rise and, by and large, triumph of scientific medicine fuelled by the development of drugs and technology has overshadowed the simpler, less glamorous but no less important basics like providing the right sort of food and drink to patients.

It was shocking to read the Audit Commission's 2001 report on hospital catering, which noted 'up to 40% of adults are either admitted to hospital with malnutrition or become malnourished during their stay.' A forthcoming Council of Europe report will tell us that 'disease-related undernutrition ... almost always becomes worse during a hospital stay.' Malnutrition and dehydration in our hospitals are damning and damaging our society. Hungry and thirsty patients may become apathetic and depressed, they may lose muscle function and become at greater risk of lung infection. Reduced mobility brings a greater likelihood of thrombo-embolism and bedsores, and undernourished patients have less ability to resist infections.

Undernourished patients

Of course, there are more or less adequate explanations for this situation related to both public health issues – like the poor quality diets of large portions of the population – and the general loss of appetite caused by disease, particularly chronic disease. However, the idea that undernourishment should persist or indeed even develop in hospital must be a call to action, as should the emerging body of evidence which suggests that better nutrition leads to better patient morale and potentially less drug use. More attention to food may lead to less money spent on antibiotics and may also result in shorter hospital stays.

The debate about the role of catering in the healing process is at last doing more than just simmering. Beginning with the King's Fund 1992 report, *A Positive Approach to Nutrition as*

Treatment, there has been a succession of publications including the Nuffield Trust's *Managing Nutrition in Hospital, Hospital Food as Treatment* published by the British Association for Parenteral and Enteral Nutrition (BAPEN) and, earlier this year, the Royal College of Physicians' *Nutrition and Patients – A Doctor's Responsibility*. There is an increasing articulation that hospital food must be seen as an integral part of effective health-care. Good catering – the right food served at the right time at the right temperature – shouldn't be a frill or a bonus, but something that has to be embedded in the working of every hospital in the country.

The NHS Plan that Alan Milburn, the Secretary of State for Health, announced in July 2000 made a clear commitment to better hospital catering. There is now a growing recognition of the role good catering can play, there is the political will to make the necessary changes that will improve catering in the NHS and there is an increasingly agreed philosophy that healthcare must become more patient centred. Why then has it taken so long to begin to change hospital catering for the better?

There are a number of cultural, technical and practical barriers to progress and change associated with the NHS and, until these barriers are fully understood and dismantled, progress will be slow. The overwhelming characteristic of the NHS is its size and scale: one million employees; 300 million meals served a year; and a catering budget in the neighbour-hood of half a billion pounds. Such gigantism isn't necessarily the enemy of change, but it certainly can slow things down. There is also the fact that the NHS was conceived in the 1940s for the conditions that were foreseeable in the 1940s and at a time when rationing was still in force. So I think the framers of the NHS can perhaps be forgiven for not having put catering at the forefront of their priorities. Catering standards and status were further eroded by years of draconian compet-itive tendering which lowered morale, reduced budgets and institutionalised a 'cheapest is best' mindset.

The NHS Plan, and the Better Hospital Food Programme that it spawned, give catering a chance to emerge from the neglect of past decades. The Plan calls for 24-hour access to food and drink for patients, a menu which is easy to read and understand, better-tasting dishes using fresher, higher-quality ingredients and the addition of two new snacks a day to avoid the intolerably long periods between some of the meal services. These innovations are being introduced in the context of other improvements, such as the end of mixed-sex wards and better bedside communications, all of which are aimed at improving patient comfort and dignity. Individually, these improvements all make good sense; taken together, they reflect a major shift in the way the NHS is responding to what patients want. They are, of course, just the beginning of a long process that I hope will introduce a series of sustainable, permanent improvements into every aspect of NHS catering.

Much of what the Better Hospital Food Programme is doing is driven by a hard-headed appreciation of how better catering can make a positive contribution to faster recovery times and lower drug costs, and much is driven by the need to reflect the significant changes in society that have taken place since the birth of NHS catering. These changes include the so-called 'food revolution' in this country and changes in the rhythm of our daily lives. Why, for example, should all hospital patients have to eat their main meal at midday when we know that in the outside world many people prefer to eat their most substantial meal in the evening? Those patients who can get out of bed to eat should do so. They should not only be allowed, but encour- aged to enjoy their meals in social situations (namely off ward) in the company of family and friends. A number of hospitals are now testing protected mealtimes – a system in which all but the most vital clinical procedures will take place at times other than mealtimes, giving patients and staff a chance to concentrate on the importance of eating in peace. Multiculturalism also has many implications for hospital menus and compared with many other countries the NHS has been extraordinarily adept at catering for a wide range of ethnic and religious dietary requirements.

Catering within the context of the NHS is like no other form of catering. Kitchens and customers are often ridiculously far apart and, uniquely, the challenge isn't just to get the food from the kitchen to the patient; it's to get the food from the kitchen *into* the patient. Many patients have low appetite levels and varying degrees of difficulty with eating, ranging from the young man with broken hands from a motorbike accident to older patients who may have difficulty swallowing.

The headline targets of the Better Hospital Food Programme are a promising start to the promotion of change. There is still a tremendous amount of work to do, but I have noticed a massive groundswell of enthusiasm within the NHS to make these changes happen. Effective communication and involvement with patients, doctors, nursing staff, caterers and all other citizens is of paramount importance. So far, the Better Hospital Food team has met with over 3000 NHS managers. There is a website explaining the programme, and a video showing how patients' food service needs should be met will follow in spring 2003.

But there are barriers to overcome. The explosive growth of the tourism and restaurant industry over the past decade has put tremendous pressure on catering staff and the recruitment and retention of talented staff has to be a main priority. Then there's the issue of water. Quite simply, NHS patients don't get enough of it and the cost of dehydration is significant. Can we replace those unwieldy jugs of water with something better that will encourage patients to drink more? There are a range of issues to address and problems to tackle. There is no one-off solution and a constant commitment is needed. The NHS has the potential to affect many aspects of food procurement and production in this country; after all, no one in the UK spends more on food than the NHS. This potential has been recognised by the Sustainability Commission and presents a whole new set of future agendas that must influence how we think about the style and method of feeding NHS patients.

The fact that there is so much to do shouldn't deter and hasn't deterred us from making a start and I believe that we are already beginning to see the results of a commitment to better, more sympathetic, more intelligent catering in Britain's Health Service.

Loyd Grossman is a writer and broadcaster with particular interests in food, the historic environment and museums and galleries. He is a commissioner of English Heritage, a member of the board of Resource: The Council for Museums, Archives and Libraries, and Chairman of the NHS Better Hospital Food Panel.

Recipe for peace: the role of nutrition in social behaviour

The prison service should act on evidence that a nutritious and healthy diet can drastically reduce criminal behaviour

Bernard Gesch

Human beings are part of the food chain, not independent from it. Thus, we are what we eat and, if we can finally accept that mind and body are not separate, a simple explanation as to why food may affect behaviour is found in the existence of the human brain which, like any other part of the body, requires nourishment in order to function normally. The brain is a metabolic powerhouse which, despite being only 2 per cent of our body mass, consumes around 20 per cent of available energy; to metabolise this energy requires a range of nutrients, vitamins, minerals and essential fatty acids. These nutrients are classed as *essential* for the normal functioning of the brain, which means there may be consequences if we do not obtain sufficient nutrients from our diet. Nutrition is a meeting point of the physical and social worlds: the hardware and software of life, so to speak, where both are required for social behaviour. Nutrition thus contains aspects of both nature and nurture. With the arrival of the awareness that nutrition may play an important role in shaping our social behaviour comes hope in the form of promising methods of rehabilitation and prevention of antisocial behaviour.

Central to any criminal justice system is the notion that someone can be held culpable for an offence where the degree of blame or individual liability is judged in addition to guilt. Discovering the causal factors that lead to differing propensities to offend will inform the degree of culpability. So to be tough on crime it makes good sense to be tough on these causes but it may also be helpful if we *knew what they were*. While nutrition is widely accepted to influence long-term health, we somehow manage to de-couple that relationship from the assumption that our behaviour is a matter of free will. Recently published research demonstrating that nutrition may be a causal factor in antisocial behaviour adds to doubts about the tenability of that assumption and suggests that, like health, our behaviour is influenced by both social and physical factors. We have identified many factors that correlate with offending but it is extremely hard to scientifically demonstrate a causal factor with societal research, as this requires rigorous experimental designs. An advantage with nutrition is that it can readily be tested in this way.

In 1942, Dr Hugh Sinclair persuaded the wartime British government to supplement the diet of all pregnant mothers and children with cod liver oil and orange juice because he had found low blood levels of many vitamins and essential fatty acids, and speculated that this might lead to a variety of ills, including antisocial behaviour. In 1971, Professor Derek Bryce-Smith published evidence that linked exposure to lead (a neurotoxin and nutrient antagonist) with antisocial behaviour. Since an individual so affected couldn't normally sense a lack of nutrients or exposure to neurotoxins, Bryce-Smith proposed that there could be potent effects on our behaviour that (unlike alcohol) *act without our knowledge*. Therefore, if an individual is unwittingly undermined by poor nutrition, those around him or her are unlikely to know about it either and would tend to attribute any inappropriate behaviour to deficits in that person's personality.

There is now a substantial body of evidence to support the existence of the effects proposed by Sinclair and Bryce-Smith. Nutrition has been demonstrated to significantly reduce antisocial behaviour with various degrees of sophistication from dietary education and the replacement of unhealthy snack foods in prisons through to double blind placebo controlled studies using nutritional supplements. There is also an abundance of evidence of the role of essential nutrients in metabolic pathways that hints at how these effects occur. Despite the immediate implications for rehabilitation and culpability, typically these factors are still not incorporated into correctional programmes for offenders or taken into account in criminal justice.

Nutritional rehabilitation

Based on this evidence, the charity Natural Justice obtained the cooperation of the Home Office to conduct an empirical study to test if poor nutrition is a cause of antisocial behaviour. This required a rigorous experimental design and was undertaken in a maximum security establishment. On a random basis, where neither the volunteers, prison staff nor researchers in the prison knew who was getting which type, 231 volunteers were given either placebo or real capsules broadly containing our daily requirements of vitamins, minerals and essential fatty acids. The number of proven offences committed by each participant was monitored; the result was that the volunteers who received the extra nutrients committed an average of 26.3 per cent fewer offences compared to the volunteers who were taking placebos, which was statistically significant. For those volunteers consuming real supplements for a minimum of two weeks, the reduction was 37 per cent for the most serious offences, such as violence, whereas those taking placebos showed little change in their propensity to offend. The differences in the rate of offending between the active and placebo groups was huge and yet could not be explained by ethnic or social factors, or variations in the administration of governor reports, etc. as they were controlled for by the randomised design; so it had to be the nutrients in the capsules that caused the change in behaviour. The participants did not guess accurately what sort of capsules they had been given either, so the importance of Bryce-Smith's idea becomes clear; here we have a potent effect on behaviour that can be measured but not sensed.

These findings will need to be retested by further studies, but we may have finally demonstrated a causal factor in antisocial behaviour. What would the future have held for these 231 young men if they had grown up with better nourishment? Sadly, we don't know but it bears thinking about.

A social time bomb

These findings have potentially far-reaching consequences as vitamins, minerals and fatty acids are essential, irrespective of location, so you would expect to see this effect in a community where poor diets are consumed: hence, it is not where you eat that is important but what you eat. One of the most scientifically intriguing aspects of this study is that the prisoners received three meals a day and, despite making poor food choices, their diets were possibly better than those consumed by many young men of the same age in the community, yet the improvement in behaviour from boosting prisoners' diets was huge. We have limited knowledge of what the optimum ranges of nutrients are from a behavioural perspective but an implication is that a great number of young people could be undermined by what they eat.

Couple this with the estimate that we may have 2 million children living in food poverty in the UK and dietary standards that currently do not take behaviour into account, and a potential social time bomb is apparent. Because nutrition is fundamental for life, its effects are pervasive and, in this context, behavioural problems we think are due to social influences, such as parenting style, may partly be down to what we eat. It is apparent that, on a societal scale, these problems are liable to be greatly amplified as greater numbers of social interactions are subject to these hitherto unnoticed influences on our behaviour that may even shift the socially acceptable norms of behaviour without our knowledge. It may sound far-fetched but few would have predicted the potency of effect shown in the prison study.

Nutrition will also interact with important social factors such as poverty, stress and the fragmentation of family but we will interpret these events entirely in terms of what we can see. Such physiological factors may turn out be important in understanding tragic and irrational acts which defy a rational explanation. It is not suggested that nutrition is the only explanation of antisocial behaviour, only that it might form a significant part. Awareness offers hope because if this scenario is correct, this process can be reversed if we choose to nourish our children rather than condemn them for influences on their behaviour that we have not taken into account.

A role for nutrition in changing societal patterns of antisocial behaviour?

If nutrition plays a causal role in our behaviour, then effects from nutrition would not only have to be in force within individuals – as has been demonstrated experimentally – but presumably should be capable of helping shape patterns of social behaviour. In the case of antisocial behaviour, these changes are considerable: according to the Criminal Statistics for England and Wales (1997), notifiable (broadly, more serious) offences have risen from 1,100 per 100,000 people in 1950 to 9,400 per 100,000 in 1996. Such changes would be hard to explain in terms of genetics, for instance, but there is evidence that changes in nutrition have occurred over the past 50 years.

A study comparing diets consumed in 1950 by 4-year-old children with those in 1992–3 concluded that the postwar diet with its reliance on staple foodstuffs, such as bread and vegetables, might well have been beneficial to the health of young people. Thus, the increase of choice and processed foods nowadays is not necessarily beneficial from a nutritional perspective. The nutritional qualities of staple foods may also have altered. The nutritional values of fruit and vegetables are significantly lower in many cases in the updated fifth edition of 1991[1] than those first published in 1936 in the seminal McCance and Widdowson's *The Nutritive Value of Fruits, Vegetables and Nuts*[2], apparently because 'the nutritional value of many of the more traditional foods has changed.' In addition, the balance of nutrients consumed may also have shifted over time with reductions in omega-3 fish oil consumption and a concomitant increase in intakes of omega-6 fatty acids; a trend that is now considered to have serious implications for mental health. It has to be recognised, however, that such historical data have limitations and the connection with changing social patterns over the past 50 years is speculative. Nevertheless, these studies do raise the possibility that such nutritional influences could have increased their grip at a time when social behaviour has deteriorated.

Curiously, there is a relatively stable feature in patterns of

1 Holland B, Welch AA, Unwin ID et al, 1991, McCance and Widdowson's *The Composition of Foods*, 5th edn, Royal Society of Chemistry and Ministry of Agriculture, Fisheries and Food, Cambridge.
2 McCance RA, Widdowson EM and Shackleton LRB, 1936, *The nutritive value of fruits, vegetables and nuts*, Medical Research Council Special Report Series No 213, HMSO, London.

crime, where the peak ages of offending are found to be consistent in different cultures among boys in late adolescence. We know that boys have a greatly accelerated growth in late adolescence while girls' growth is more linear. This is only speculation, but perhaps this is the only time when the developed brain is in such competition with the rest of the body for precious nutrients that their behavioural influences may conceivably reach a peak during the growth spurt, then tail off.

Conclusion

The brain needs to be nourished in two ways: the love, nurturing and education we all need, but also the nutrition to sustain our physical being. Some of these factors will act in ways that we can see, some of them *will not*; thus, we need a broader interpretation of the causes of antisocial behaviour in criminal justice, where physical and social functioning are both considered relevant to culpability. Clinical studies suggest that nutrition is cheap, humane and highly effective at reducing anti-social behaviour. Most important, people's positive potential might be realised if such an approach were taken at a time when criminal justice resources are under stress. To make an analogy, no amount of energy spent on software will resolve a hardware problem. If this physiological approach works, it should work irrespective of racial, legislative or geographical boundaries, as human metabolism unites us all. Given the possible benefits, more research is urgently needed.

Nature offers us a clue about the way forward by providing natural foodstuffs that grow in harmony with their environment and invariably contain a range of nutrients in dosages to which our metabolism is attuned. It should come as no surprise, therefore, that vitamins, minerals and essential fatty acids all seem to have protective effects on antisocial behaviour, particularly those nutrients that modern practices have rendered less available. We need to develop our understanding of the dosage and range of nutrients required to positively impact on behaviour. It may be a recipe for peace.

Bernard Gesch is a Senior Research Scientist in the Department of Physiology, University of Oxford, and Director of the research charity Natural Justice, which investigates causes of antisocial behaviour.

Urban agriculture in Australia: local food, global communities

Local food networks need a strong policy narrative to transform communities

John Brisbin

In Uganda, *urban agriculture* means preventing starvation amongst single mothers and their families in the ruined fringes of Kampala. For Berliners, it means affluent, lifelong city-dwellers celebrating cherished cultural traditions in their immaculate *Schrebergärten*. In Australia, urban agriculture might refer to an inner-city community garden, a suburban farmers market, or a bountiful backyard kitchen garden.

These experiences of urban/peri-urban agriculture (UPA) seem worlds apart, yet they all share at least one important feature: they serve to bring the living processes of food and community into a local focus. Wherever urban agriculture is found, its underlying concern is the interweaving of growers with growing, and eaters and eating to form a web of physical and social connections that maximise benefits with least effort. The dynamics of UPA systems can be described more generally as *local food networks*. Joining people to each other and to the land, these networks encompass the practical aspects of cultivation, harvest and distribution and, more importantly, the social dimension of shared experience. Powered by frisson at the urban/rural boundary, UPA issues can enliven vital social discourse in the developed world. The urban farm visionary Jac Smit observes:

> *Farming in the open spaces of a community brings a community together. Farming requires coopera-tion/partnership and creates community. Perhaps the greatest benefit in the 21st century of urban farming will turn out to be its capacity to reconnect urban [wo/]man with nature.*

I suggest that urban agriculture can be an effective, localised community-building mechanism among the urban and suburban middle class. Further, a strong public policy and implementation framework can help position UPA as a generator of positive cultural narratives, which promote a personal engagement with environmental sustainability. This social transformation, achieved through *community building*, can lead to important changes in lifestyle and consumption patterns in a developed nation such as Australia. A secondary effect of this is the reduction of structural pressures on the poor and hungry, who are the typical focus of UPA initiatives.

Raising the game

We are concerned here with the potential to raise the moral and creative capacity of a society. Local food networks are ideal structures to carry information about living in balance with the environment and with one another. Connections are re-estab-lished. In the UK, this connectivity was identified as the key cultural outcome in the 'Future of Farming' White Paper:

> *Our central theme is reconnection. We believe the real reason why the present situation [in food policy] is so dysfunctional is that farming has become detached from the rest of the economy and the environment.*
> *The key objective of public policy should be to reconnect our food and farming industry: to*

reconnect farming with its market and the rest of the food chain; to reconnect the food chain and the countryside; and to reconnect consumers with what they eat and how it is produced.[1]

The few extant surveys of Australian urban farm and garden activity reveal a surprising level of public participation yet, in terms of cultural story,[2] the existence of such activity is largely unspoken. We have very few positive images of city farming, office food swapping, downtown co-ops, etc. There is no visionary story, or 'policy narrative'[3] to inform public discourse. Local food networks are a popular story waiting to be told.

Local food networks typically find expression as:

- farmers markets
- farm gate trails
- food co-ops
- community supported agriculture (CSA)
- community gardens
- family/backyard gardens
- seed saving groups
- school gardens

These networks are often 'powered' by one or two key individuals, facilitator/leaders who are the human attractors responsible for stirring the motions of community into being. Empowering and assisting these individuals is the critical strategy for creating more local food networks.

Alternative economies

Aggressive public participation in local food networks could begin with the design and deployment of public policies that foster local food networks. However, direct civil support of UPA runs contrary to the dominant economic paradigm in developed countries. UPA promotes local self-sufficiency manifested in fungible transactions, ie non-cash value exchange (through barter, charity, common bounty, etc).[4] Commercial operators, who see the cashless operations of local food networks as a direct threat to their business, fiercely challenge

1 Cabinet Office, Jan 2002 [http://www.cabinet-office.gov.uk/farming].
2 Julian Rappaport discusses the form and function of story extensively. He asserts that stories are critical components of cultural behaviour because 'stories mimic the way we actually experience the world – as sequential, woven interrelationships experienced in real time. Stories about our people, our community, and our settings are particularly powerful vehicles to influence our possible selves', 'The art of social change', 1998, in XB Arriaga and S Oskamp (eds) *Addressing community problems*, p 240.
3 For more discussion of policy narratives, see the excellent book by Emery Roe, 1994, *Narrative policy analysis: theory and practice*, Duke University Press, Durham NC.
4 The UNDP recognises the benefits of non-cash economies [http://www.awd.org.au/urbanagr.htm].

government and community projects of any size. Since there is no thread of analysis that informs policy attached to local food networks, public intervention in the food business can be portrayed as a frontal attack on free markets. This lack of a coherent guiding principle is dangerous territory for committed politicians and policymakers alike. They are likely to see the policy rubbished rather than accepted.

Failure to develop a relevant social narrative that celebrates UPA as a groovy middle-class preoccupation means that UPA will remain a 'concern of the poor'. Efforts to engender enthusiasm for sustainable cities via integrated agriculture will inevitably be understood as prescriptive and exclusionary. Community gardens will be forever associated with the underprivileged and therefore off the dominant cultural agenda. We in the middle class will lose the opportunity to community-build around a positive, life-affirming activity.

I believe that, under favourable conditions, local food networks will form spontaneously. The social and economic perceptions that can be shaped by individuals, community groups and NGOs can be sufficient to achieve localised success despite the lack of a mainstream social narrative. Essentially, any feedback mechanism that positively reinforces the clustering of supply and demand for local produce via an alternative food system will yield emergent results. The US-based Community Gardens Association has even developed a curriculum for optimising the social outputs from garden projects.[5]

Australian Community Foods[6] offers a case study in self-instantiating behaviours. It is an experiment with positive feedback mechanisms promoting community networking and effective group management. Access to the website is available free of charge for anyone interested in local food, including growers, retailers, co-ops and, of course, the people who consume food. The facility is built around a geo-spatial directory and matching service. Users fill out a short profile form and their directory entry is geo-coded. Each month, the directory database is analysed to find matching profiles (correlations are based on geography and user preferences). A server-side agent sends out email introductions to the people listed in

5 http://www.communitygarden.org/pubs/index.html
6 http://www.communityfoods.com.au

the directory. The site allows anonymous contacts to be initiated between parties so that privacy preferences are respected. The long-term effect of this introduction service will be quietly and steadily to invite local community connections that might not have occurred otherwise.

Equally important is the lowering of barriers to participation. As noted earlier, local food networks are often powered by individuals with a passion for their cause. However, the work of community-building involves a range of skills, including the capacity to support administrative functions associated with group formation and maintenance.

Our observations in Australia have shown that, for many growers and consumers, this administrative load is simply too much of an additional burden. As a result, alternative food systems generally present a fractured, poorly articulated experience. When an isolated success does occur, the lack of a robust information-sharing network means that a valuable solution pattern is not widely communicated to others.

The web can be an ally in this struggle and Australian Community Foods is working to demonstrate some potentially useful applications through the website, including a mix of facilities to meet typical community-building demands:

- self-publishing to encourage local content accumulation
- site hosting for organisations without an existing website
- online tools to streamline group interaction (eg newsletter creation) and contacts management

Our progress, as the site is rolled out nationally, will provide valuable experience to others seeking to grow strong community connections in the alternative food supply chain. Although Australian Community Foods has only just been launched (Oct 2002), it has attracted significant interest from major growers, government and consumer associations. In the US, Local Harvest could be seen as a more mature cousin of our Australian endeavour.[7]

Morag Gamble, one of Australia's leading city farm champions, eloquently affirms the benefits of local food networks:

7 http://www.localharvest.org

Community-led urban agriculture projects facilitate positive change on many levels. The projects not only help to create a sense of place and ownership, but help to strengthen ties between community members, between residents and their local environment, and between residents and the regional businesses, institutions and governing bodies.[8]

8 [http://www.regiona l.org.au/au/soc/2002/3 /gamble.htm]

Through a combination of positive feedback dynamics and creative community-building, we hope to see Australian Community Foods add measurably to a sustainable (and sustaining) emergence of local food networks.

John Brisbin is the president of Australian Community Foods, an incorporated non-profit association providing internet technologies to support local food networks. He has been exploring networked information systems professionally and personally since the early 80s.

People – the missing ingredient

People need to know the stories of food production so they can become 'good' consumers

Daniel Miller

Story 1: sometime in the recent past – a shopping expedition
I am impressed; this is the third consumer I have talked to this week. Altruism seems alive and kicking in this particular leafy middle-class suburb of North London. I have heard about issues to do with the exploitation of farmers in developing countries, the importance of organic foods, a need for people to get a grip on themselves and think carefully about what they eat. Some quite funny stories about subtle substitutions and white lies in order to persuade husbands and children to eat healthier food than they would otherwise have done – peanut butter emerges as a real boon here. Of course, there are priorities: 'I never give out-of-date foods to my children,' one said, horrified at the thought. 'I give them to my husband!' Ok, so maybe people are a bit complacent, but at least they are conscious of what matters and why, and feel able to take positive action for the good.

The next stage in my fieldwork is to go shopping with them. My interest is in comparing what they say with what they do. This proves to be a shock. It's as though I am dealing with two entirely different people, the speaker and the person picking the products. There are fair trade products in the shop, but no-one buys any of them and actually, if the truth be told, the proportion of goods that speak to the altruism of the shoppers is minuscule in relation to the whole. Furthermore, what is becoming very clear is that the reasons behind what might have seemed like altruistic shopping are invariably selfish. Organic foods are occasionally purchased but, in the end, the concern is never with the planet at large. It is simply that there is a gnawing fear about what pesticides might do to the families of the shoppers. It is their health that ultimately determines these concerns. It is just a matter of good fortune that this can also appear to be altruistic. It covers them for both motivations.

Having observed this discrepancy, I wonder. They are talking about issues at the very moment that they do not appear to be actually acting upon them; but they don't seem particularly hypocritical. How exactly does this work? I listen to the tapes of my interviews more carefully.

How to be good

One point that emerges is that when they were talking about how good they were, there were (*pace* Nick Hornby) so many different ways to be good. Half an hour is spent discussing issues about the environment and the third world, about 'doing one's bit'. There is implied condemnation of those who used to be termed 'common' people, who don't watch their weight, who it is assumed don't show any concern for others, or the environment. The constant emphasis is on buying healthy foods for one's children and so forth. There is plenty of talk but, on second listening, it emerges that concrete altruistic actions are rare. Indeed, in some conversations, about the only specific instance of 'being good' in practice is the determination to keep a trim waistline by eating low fat foods. I can't personally see dieting doing much for the developing world. However, listening to the way both topics crop up within the same conversation, I can see how the speaker had managed to lump them all together under the general ideal of eating well and being good.

On further reflection, a more subtle problem presented itself. Howard and Willmott recently suggested[1] a conflict in consumption between altruism and self-interest, but that's not

1 Howard M and Willmott M, 2001, 'Ethical consumption in the twenty first century', in T Bentley and D Stedman Jones (eds) *The moral universe*, Demos Collection 16, London, p 118.

what emerges when accompanying shoppers. Rather, there is a conflict between two forms of altruism.

My consumers, on the whole, were a pretty unselfish lot; indeed, the housewives who dominate food shopping are generally not a group that we associate with rampant self-interest. But the love that motivated them, the care that suffused through everything they thought about and did was care for their families. What exercised their attention right through the day, even when they were at work, were the needs of their children and partners. Other ethical concerns worked best as an extension of this. First, we care about our immediate loved ones, then other people in our own society, then other societies, then the planet in general. For my consumers it was natural for issues of GM food to follow on from issues about their children not doing enough sport.

When it came to the act of shopping, however, the situation was quite different. One of the main ways these women constantly demonstrated concern for their own households was through their responsibility in managing the household budget. They prided themselves constantly on how much they saved every time they went shopping. For them, thrift was about saving the resources of the family in order to have the potential for other expenditures. Rarely was the money saved spent on themselves as individuals. It was rather an expression of their conscientiousness as the person responsible for the household. It was this factor of price that marked the difference between conversation and action. A typical remark with regard to organic vegetables as we were walking past them was 'The price of them. I maybe am a bit sensitive to price when it comes to them. I do occasionally buy them. I sometimes wonder if I should buy more.'

To be ethically concerned with the welfare of producers is to be prepared to pay more for these goods, a premium that may be a small proportion of the price at the supermarket but potentially a major difference to the wages going to the original workers. Perhaps one day ethical foods will be as cheap as exploitative foods, but this seems most unlikely. In the meantime, the practical expression of an ethical concern takes the form of spending more, which runs directly counter to the morality being expressed in thrift. It gets worse. As one listens to the opinions and comments of the shoppers, the associations that emerge in terms of saving money for one's family are those of the warm caring mother and partner. By comparison, those whose identities are bound up with reminding people about these larger distant ethical concerns are seen as relatively cold, hectoring, the 'Linda Snells' (citing 'The Archers'). Ethical consumption, which should have associations of care, is seen as a kind of moral mistake, something done by people who are so wrapped up in the larger planet or the developing world as to have neglected what they should really care about – their children. This is not what I expected, and certainly not what I wanted to find. But as they say – it explains a whole lot.

Story 2: some time in the near future – bananas, ginger beer and bacon

Right, class, I guess everyone has heard about the infestation on the St Lucian plantation, which is now under control. So there is no threat to our bananas. Good to see a close-up of the destructive effects on the webcam. As usual, our ten-minute interactive with Selwyn has been archived for anyone who missed the live session. Selwyn was making fun of our weather, as always. The infestation certainly teaches us how little you can take for granted in agricultural supply.

We have an agreement with St Mary's secondary at Westcliff. If anything happens to the bananas designated for shipment to their school, we will share ours and vice versa. That's how the supermarkets do it – they have contingency plans and a wide range of suppliers. But, of course, the situation for Selwyn and his family in St Lucia is different. They have their cooperative's support but it is quite likely that, if something serious happens to his plantation, the other families in the cooperative will also be affected.

I just want to remind you of the coming interactive events. The ginger beer bottles that we are tracking have reached a further stage. They have now left Trinidad and next week we will have a session with the people working on the container ship prior to their docking at Southampton. After that, we will hear from a supermarket manager responsible for the soft drink division. He will talk about how his firm deals with the wholesale and distribution side of things. As it happens, he is also the person who is responsible for making sure you get the bottles with your personal labels on. As for the third and final product that we are studying, we will go interactive with John's dad who will explain to you the kinds of work you might be involved in if you look for future employment in our local agricultural sector. Over the next few weeks, we will meet secretarial, management and cleaning staff in the food distribution sector. You can post advanced questions onto our website during the break. Also on the website is a breakdown of the prices we pay at supermarkets, and you can see how each penny is allocated to distinct costs, such as shipping, labelling, advertising. They have also given us a sheet of other factors that we should know about, because of the consequences for them. These include the effect of changes in the value of supermarket land and the cost of fuel for transport. All of this will be covered in our 'real economies' class within the geography syllabus. It is important you look at this carefully since in the exam you may well be expected to make up a plausible version of these components of price. For homework, I want you also to compare the 'consumers' rights' and the 'consumer responsibilities' sections on the national website.

I hope, by now, you are gaining a sense of the life story of our three chosen products and the lives of people involved in these processes. We can't go into this amount of detail for every product you buy. As I have told you, a strawberry yoghurt pot may include materials from a dozen different places once we start looking at plastics, foil, fruit, and so forth. But you will know that they all have their own story and that every time you buy something you are part of that story. We hear that, next year, schools in Trinidad will be adopting the same programme. They have been waiting for their schools to have the right broadband access but that is now in place. They will be following products made here in the UK that they buy in supermarkets over there. John's dad has agreed to continue to coordinate a contribution to the programme on local packing of bacon, so by then some of your families will be appearing on interactive sessions as employees to school children in Trinidad, just as their parents have been guiding us through their work.

Beyond fetishism

While the popularity of Marx's writings has fluctuated wildly over the last two decades, one essential concern of his work seems to have been little altered by such debates: the idea of fetishism, ie that commodities appear as the outcome of capital rather than the labour of people. Indeed, given that most production is today so far removed from us as consumers, this problem has probably increased rather than reduced since his time. The old videos of chocolate making that pupils used to watch in school geography lessons provided images of plantation workers, but they seemed so distant from us and, in the next frame, the chocolate appeared on the supermarket shelves. But de-fetishising foods requires much more than this. We need teaching to become an experience of living within an economy. Goods need to be followed through as narratives that include the lives of packers, shippers, secretaries, store managers, processing sheds. We need this to include local food production so that children see workers as people they also will become, not just the population of the developing world.

In my studies of shopping in London, I found that there was a conversation readily available for raising and addressing ethical concerns but, as I have suggested, this was rarely applied to the actual act of purchasing. We need something more radical and more practical to turn that conversation into a change in action. In short, we need our relationship to food as consumers to always implicate our relationship to food as producers and distributors. There has been an increase in the teaching of economics, but it is dominated by the more abstract modelling that trickles down from university teaching, not a sense of the experience of working as an economic agent – not what we might call 'real economies'. I cannot promise that this kind of de-fetishising (that is, ensuring that we all grow up with a consciousness of food production and processing) will necessarily result in the other form of de-fetishising (that is, the full reward of labour for its place in these processes) but it is likely to be a step in that direction. In the meantime, I do feel sure that people cannot be called educated when they remain in ignorance of the consequences of their daily actions as consumers.

Daniel Miller teaches anthropology at University College London. The ideas in this paper may be found in expanded form in A Theory of Shopping *(Polity, 1998);* The Dialectics of Shopping *(Chicago University Press, 2001); and in 'Could the Internet De-fetishise the Commodity?',* Environment and Planning D Society and Space.

Part 4

Global hunger

The rich diet, and the poor go hungry

Tackling hunger means tackling poverty, not distributing OECD food surpluses to poor countries

Clare Short

Why is it that, despite unprecedented economic growth in the second half of the twentieth century, one half of the world suffers diseases from over-eating and the other half lie down for the night hungry? The world produces more than enough food for every man, woman and child and yet, in many countries, more and more people are unable to obtain enough to feed themselves.

In 1993, the UN Food and Agriculture Organisation (FAO) estimated that 840 million people in the world did not have enough to eat. Two-thirds of the world's absolute poor – mainly women and children – remain food insecure.[1] Since then, the number has been reduced by about 20 million.[2] A closer look at the State of Food Insecurity Report (FAO, 2002) reveals an even more alarming fact; the modest reduction in hunger is the result of rapid progress in very few countries, notably China. In 47 countries, hunger has actually increased. Despite questions about the accuracy of measurement, the message is loud and clear – progress is far too slow to meet either the Millennium Development Goal on hunger or the more ambitious World Food Summit target.[3]

[1] Food security describes a situation in which people have physical, social and economic access to sufficient, safe and nutritious food that meets their dietary needs and food preferences for an active and healthy life.

[2] The State of Food Insecurity Report, 2002, FAO, Rome.

[3] At the Millennium Summit in 2000, 149 countries resolved to halve the *proportion* of people who suffer from hunger, a redefinition of the 1996 World Food Summit's target to halve the *number* of people who are hungry by 2015.

Each year, malnutrition is a key factor in the deaths of more than 6 million children under the age of five. Malnutrition and micronutrient deficiencies also cause widespread disease (such as vitamin A deficiency causing blindness in children) and impair millions of people's ability to resist and recover from infections. It has a crippling effect on people's mental and physical development as well as their ability to learn and to work. A recent study by the Asian Development Bank estimated that the combined effects of three common forms of malnutrition (stunting, iodine and iron deficiencies) reduce GDP on average by 2–4 per cent per year.

Why, when the world produces ample food, do so many people still go hungry? And why, despite decades of development effort, are we still unable to satisfy this basic human need and fundamental right to food? Both questions are important to me, not only in my role as Secretary of State for International Development but as a member of a party which is committed to social justice at home and abroad. We need to understand why we haven't made sufficient progress up until now in order to make better progress in future.

Hunger – a question of food availability or access?

Hunger is the pain from lack of food. The simplistic answer to this is to provide food by increasing food production. This simplistic approach is to blame for the unacceptably slow progress we have made so far. If food alone is the problem, why do people go hungry in countries that are self-sufficient in food production, whilst other countries that are not self-sufficient in food, feed all their people? Hunger is much more to do with people's *ability* to obtain food than with food availability.

Although the world has so far managed to produce enough food to keep pace with population growth and rising demand, we have done little to improve poor people's access to food. We need to understand better the multidimensionality of hunger; who is hungry and why. We need to relate hunger to poor people's livelihoods and the risks and vulnerabilities that affect them.

Poverty, poor health, social and economic exclusion, conflict and natural disasters, poor public policies and weak governance are all causes of hunger. Poverty, however, is the main cause of hunger.

Poverty is multidimensional; economic, social, political and cultural factors all play a part in keeping people poor. We recognise that the rules guiding behaviour within a culture, the policies regulating opportunities and addressing security and justice or governing trade and international relations all influence how people forge livelihoods for themselves. Local or global economic shocks, conflicts or natural disasters determine the degree to which people's livelihoods flourish or decline. We must be much more proficient at identifying *who* is poor, and why, and work harder to understand how this complex web of interrelationships frames their poverty.

Any attempt to help people to escape poverty and hunger must rest on supporting their livelihood strategies and must take into account that 'tugging one part of the web' will affect the rest.

Therefore, to address hunger we need to address the causes of poverty and the underlying vulnerability of the poor. Developing countries with strong economic growth and good social policies are making the biggest impact on hunger. How is it that some countries have managed to reduce hunger whereas in others the number of hungry people is increasing? When we analyse the reasons for slow progress, we discover the usual suspects: unhelpful macro-economic policies, poor governance and the shocks resulting from HIV/AIDS, armed conflict and natural disasters. All of these factors impact on the viability of people's livelihoods and, therefore, on whether they are likely to suffer hunger.

Globalisation and trade

Globalisation is leading to greater interdependence and connectedness between people and states. Increased global trade is integrating global markets in goods and services, and increasing competitive pressures. Whether poor people will become winners or losers as a result of globalisation depends largely on how well national governmental policies and international trade agreements are able to assure their access to fair markets, goods and services. Globalisation will expose small rural producers to price volatility and risk as rural areas become more integrated into global markets. The ability of these households to cope will depend on trade and other policies pursued by national and other governments.

Many developments in international trade have implications for food security: for example, changes in market access, export subsidies, domestic support and trade preferences. As trade policies evolve, we must ensure that they work for the poor. Trade barriers can bring developing-country industries to their knees. Applied tariffs, for example, are sometimes higher than 100 per cent for agricultural goods, and non-tariff barriers, such as unjustifiably high food standards, can be just as powerful in blocking competition from poorer countries. Agricultural products and labour-intensive items, such as textiles and clothing, are the most important exports of developing countries. Cutting the very high tariffs and the agricultural support provided in developed countries (an estimated US$327 billion in 2000) would help to boost agricultural exports from developing countries, although the benefits will not be seen overnight. According to World Bank estimates, cutting tariffs by half in both developed and developing countries would bring gains of US$150 billion to developing countries. Interestingly, this is about three times the amount that these countries receive in development aid.

The rural–urban divide is fading

Earlier strategies to reduce hunger focused more on the symptoms of hunger than on generating sustainable economic growth. They largely failed to consider risk and vulnerability. Although agriculture will remain the engine for economic growth in many countries, agricultural and other policies cannot afford to ignore the changes that are sweeping through rural areas and transforming their economies. Rural and urban growth is increasingly linked with migration and commuting between rural and urban areas. Food security is no longer mainly a rural problem. A recent assessment in Russia showed that food insecurity is more prevalent in urban than rural areas.

Diversified livelihood strategies are becoming more important than agriculture in many rural areas. Migrant urban dwellers send money home to rural areas, which is reinvested. Failure to support positive economic changes with appropriate policies that encourage mobility and rural diversification will impact on poverty and, therefore, on hunger.

Health is a major influence on food security. Sick adults are less able to provide for their families and to care for children. Diseases that affect adults, such as HIV/AIDS, tuberculosis and malaria, seriously limit the ability of householders, communities and governments to tackle hunger. HIV/AIDS, in particular, predominantly affects the age group that is most economically active. Families affected by HIV/AIDS are forced to spend savings and sell assets to purchase food and medicines. The need to care for ailing household members further constrains the work capacity and income-earning ability of other family members who are not ill. In turn, food insecurity contributes to the spread of HIV/AIDS. Privation can drive women and children into the sex trade, accelerating a downward spiral of poverty, food insecurity and disease.

Education and nutrition are also closely linked to health, livelihoods and food security. Education is the key to finding more productive and better-paid employment and breaking out of the poverty trap. Better-educated women understand the importance of care practices, such as breastfeeding, weaning and hygiene, and tend to feed their children better. Improving women's education has reduced child malnutrition by 40 per cent over the past 25 years. Food insecurity is an obstacle to education, nutrition and health, since households that are food-insecure tend to take their children out of school and spend less time on care and feeding of their children. It is therefore critically important to recognise how health and educational policies interact with nutrition and food security to influence the household (and by extension, the national) economy.

Conflict and food security

No discussion of food security can afford to ignore the growing problem of conflict – the major cause in 15 of the 44 countries that suffered exceptional food emergencies in 2001. In the Democratic Republic of Congo, conflict and the resulting political and economic crises have almost doubled the proportion of undernourished people to 64 per cent of the population since 1990. Conflict disrupts lives and livelihoods, destroys societies and economies and reduces access to basic services. According to FAO, conflict in sub-Saharan Africa alone between 1970 and 1997 resulted in losses of almost $52 billion in agricultural output. This is equivalent to 75 per cent of all official development assistance to these conflict-affected countries for that period. Most wars now take place in the poorest countries and within states rather than between them. Most of their victims are poor people. A priority, therefore, for the international community must be resolving existing conflicts and defusing potential flashpoints.

How should we respond to food crises?

Erratic rainfall and drought can be identified as contributing factors to acute vulnerability but in many cases the causes of the (current) crisis can be linked to other sources. Serious problems of governance, weakened social sectors, poorly performing or constrained private sectors and poor macroeconomic performance are seriously affecting key countries in the region. Worst of all, Southern Africa is being devastated by the HIV/AIDS pandemic. HIV/AIDS is a fundamental, underlying cause of vulnerability in the region.

These were the conclusions of a recent report (Morris, Sept 2002) by the Special Envoy of the UN Secretary General for Humanitarian Needs in Southern Africa. Many of the food crises we currently see, whether in North Korea, Afghanistan or Southern Africa, are not only a result of natural disasters such as drought or floods. The underlying causes of the crises are often more to do with conflict, economic mismanagement, poor governance or inappropriate policies on trade, markets and access to land.

In the short term, appropriate use of food aid will address the immediate needs of the hungry but we also need to address the underlying causes. This means strong political commitment and honesty both by affected countries and the international community to tackle these more difficult and sensitive issues if we are to succeed.

The role of food aid

There is, however, much disagreement about the appropriateness of food aid. The use of timely and appropriate food aid is a legitimate and valuable response to food crises; however, if food aid is appropriate, where possible, it should be sourced locally, strengthening production and local markets. Food aid is often given when there is no immediate crisis or when the crisis has passed and other forms of support or transfer, such as cash, would be more useful in rehabilitating people's livelihoods. Inappropriate food aid can undermine local production and markets.

The Food Aid Convention, set up to ensure stable and predictable minimum levels of food aid globally, has not achieved its aim. Food aid has had limited success in addressing hunger and malnutrition. Programme food aid, where food aid is monetised to provide balance of payments and budgetary support, has rarely done much to improve food security. How much food aid the developed world provides has more to do with food surpluses in OECD countries than with actual need. The Food Aid Convention needs to be reviewed and its role reassessed but this means putting vested interests aside and focusing on the needs of the hungry and the causes of food insecurity.

The challenge of tackling hunger must therefore be the challenge of tackling poverty. It is, at the same time, both deeply personal for those who are suffering, and essentially political in its causes and solutions. Accepting the challenge means getting serious about how we view our rights and responsibilities as citizens and governments of an increasingly interconnected world. It means accepting that hunger and poverty *are* our concerns and affect us all, if not today, then in the future.

Rt Hon Clare Short MP is Secretary of State for International Development and the Member of Parliament for Birmingham Ladywood.

The politics of the empty belly

Making African farming economically viable
is a step away from mass famine

Alex de Waal

In poor countries, food symbolises power, and also constitutes it. The rich and the rulers are 'eating'; the poor are 'hungry'. Nigerian novelist Chinua Achebe's account of African politics is pervaded by imagery of eating. 'Let them eat,' the people say of their rulers, 'who knows? It may be your turn to eat tomorrow.'[1] A ruler is expected to be corpulent. Thinness is a mark of the poor. In African political systems, the distribution of largesse by the ruling elites, as the prime means of managing the affairs of state, has been termed 'the politics of the belly'.[2] Controlling food systems, including food aid, is also pivotal in governments' ability to stay on top of turbulent political systems.

Meanwhile, food – or lack of it – is a powerful idiom for political protest. On occasions, the unmet demand for food can bring down governments. For example, in 1985 Sudanese President Jaafar Nimeiri's failure to respond to a major drought and famine drove citizens to take to the streets in a non-violent intifada that prompted the army to step in, depose the government, declare a national drought emergency and restore democracy. This recalls early nineteenth-century English protesters who believed that the call for a 'provisional government'

1 Achebe C, 1966, *A man of the people*, Heinemann, London, pp 161–2.
2 Bayart J-F, 1989, *L'État en Afrique: la politique du ventre*, Fayard, Paris.

was a demand for one that would supply provisions for the poor.[3]

Governments respond to famines less out of concern for their hungry citizens than for self-preservation. This is why the British imperial government in nineteenth-century India, which had formerly steadfastly held to the Malthusian principle that famine was a natural check on the subcontinent's 'over-population', was belatedly obliged to reverse its position and institute the 'Famine Codes', which remain the foundation for India's remarkably effective famine prevention system today. Food scarcities caused political unrest 100 years ago, and threaten to do so again today. The economist Jean Drèze quotes an Indian labourer working on an emergency employment scheme during a drought in Maharashtra: 'They would let us die if they thought we would not make a noise about it.'[4] The readiness of a democratic government to listen to its citizens' cries of distress is the underpinning of Amartya Sen's much-quoted remark that 'the diverse political freedoms that are available in a democratic state, including regular elections, free newspapers and freedom of speech, must be seen as the real force behind the elimination of famines [in India].'[5]

Most liberal commentators who have applauded this argument have overlooked its counterpart, also examined in detail by Sen, which is that, while democratic India has not suffered a major famine in more than half a century, its record in overcoming chronic hunger is feeble in comparison with despotic China. Chairman Mao Zedong presided over the greatest famine of the twentieth century – the 1958–61 calamity of the 'Great Leap Forward' – which cost perhaps 30 million lives and which remained a state secret until Chinese demographers investigated the unexplained shortage of young adults that followed 20 years later. However, Mao also built a rural health care and food system that delivered life expectancies comparable to the developed world. In India, several million premature deaths every year can be attributed to chronic poverty, malnutrition and lack of sanitation, all of which persist despite the democratic system.

Famine is dramatic and visible, an irruption into normality that compels an urgent response. It is an issue around which to mobilise and march, and build coalitions between the affected masses and concerned elites. It naturally ties itself into other

3 Thompson EP, 1980, *The making of the English working class*, Penguin, London, p 732.
4 Drèze J, 1990, 'Famine Prevention in India', in J Drèze and A Sen (eds) *The political economy of hunger, vol II: Famine prevention*, Clarendon Press, Oxford, p 93.
5 Sen A, 1990, 'Individual freedom as a social commitment', *New York Review of Books*, 14 Jun.

political agendas, like independence. Both Irish and Indian nationalists claimed that mass starvation was the ultimate refutation of any imperial civilising mission. Moreover, famine lends itself to deceptively simple remedies: send food, and stop over-taxing the people. But endemic hunger and poverty do not elicit the same response. Are these problems just too big and complex to be manageable? Or do the necessary responses make too many demands on the vested interests of the political establishment? Hunger usually has its beneficiaries. Bertholt Brecht remarked that 'famines do not just happen, they are organised by the grains trade.' Contemporary political science has made the same point.[6] When the hunger is chronic and systemic, combating it may be just too difficult politically.

However, for even the most autocratic and corrupt government, feeding the people remains a touchstone of legitimacy. Failure to do so tends to hand a powerful card to the political opposition which, if played, then makes food an organising issue for political life. Democratic institutions facilitate the working of this social contract, but political choices determine whether food and famine are part of the deal and, if so, in what way.[7] No country is sufficiently poor that it cannot feed itself. Famines are acts of government (and sometimes rebel armies). Until now, modern famines in Africa have been one of the following three kinds.

First are famines of neglect, indifference and chronic exploitation. Usually a drought or some other proximate cause brings down epidemic hunger on a poor and vulnerable people. Typically these famines don't kill many people. The Sahelian famine of the early 1970s witnessed no overall rise in mortality rates across the affected regions at all.[8] The mid-1980s famines in Ethiopia and Sudan did kill several hundred thousand people, mostly young children, on account of infectious diseases, but the more remarkable story about these episodes is the resilience and skill displayed by rural people in the drought-stricken areas, who managed to survive despite the collapse of local food production and late and inadequate food relief.

Second, and particularly common in the last decade, are war famines, inflicted for political and military reasons. There are subtypes: counterinsurgency famines, siege famines, famines caused by forced relocation and famines inflicted by armies

6 Keen D, 1994, *The benefits of famine: a political economy of famine in South-Western Sudan 1983–89*, Princeton University Press, Princeton NJ.

7 De Waal A, 1997, *Famine crimes: politics and the disaster relief industry in Africa*, James Currey and International African Institute, Oxford.

8 Caldwell JC, 1977, 'Demographic aspects of drought: an examination of the African drought of 1970–74', in D Dalby, R Harrison-Church and F Bezzaz (eds) *Drought in Africa 2*, International African Institute, London.

living off the land. When soldiers decide to prevent people from undertaking any economic activities, including survival strategies, then we see a different and much worse kind of famine, marked by outright starvation. The verb 'to starve' is transitive, like murder; it is something that people do to one another.

The third kind is plunder famines. This is the 'politics of the belly' taken to extremes and occurs when extractive, patrimonial or rent-seeking political–economic systems turn their predation onto the poorest or most vulnerable population. We see the dispossession of the basic means of livelihood (eg by land confiscation, raiding of livestock, looting of food stores) and also stealing food aid. They differ from war famines in that the motivation of the famine-mongers is primarily economic, rather than political or military.

Today we are also seeing the emergence of a fourth variant, which partly overlaps with the others. This is the HIV/AIDS-related famine – a new type, instigated by the ways in which the massive human losses caused by the pandemic render societies more vulnerable to shocks and less resilient in coping with them. While recovery from peacetime famines is usually rapid, full recovery from an AIDS famine may be impossible.

The current food crisis in Southern Africa is unprecedented in modern history. It threatens a peace-time famine, whose proximate cause is drought, eminently predictable because of the regular 10- or 11-year rainfall cycle in the region, but which has not only overwhelmed the established responses of governments and communities, but is escalating at a bewildering rate. The reason for this is that HIV/AIDS strikes adults in their most productive years and all Southern African countries have adult populations with HIV rates of 15 per cent or more – well over 30 per cent in several cases. The human resource losses due to AIDS are transforming all aspects of Southern African society, resulting in this new strain of famine. While agrarian societies have adapted well to the stresses of a 'traditional' drought famine, this ability to cope relies heavily on the survival and continued hard work of adults. In communities that have lost a quarter or more of their young women and men to the disease, these survival strategies are no longer possible. How can what is called a 'sibling household' – the surviving children of a family in which the parents are dead –

have the skills and labour necessary for the tasks of gathering wild foods and migrating to find casual employment? The success of famine survival strategies also falls disproportionately on women, but HIV typically infects young women in their teens or early 20s – years younger than men. Increasingly, it is feared that Southern Africa's AIDS-related food crisis will lead to rampant frank starvation on a scale never seen before.

Africa also gets an unfair deal in an unforgiving global economic system. Too often it is the victim of both the rich world's protectionism and insistence on (selective) free trade. The protection of agricultural markets in Europe and North America costs Africa dear. If Africa could achieve just a 1 per cent increase in its share of world exports, the net annual financial inflow to the continent would be about $70 billion.[9] Compare this with the current total aid flows of about $10 billion. Compare it also to the 'finance gap' identified by the New Partnership for Africa's Development initiative, which is $50–64 billion which, if met from both domestic and international sources (investment, aid and debt relief), would make it possible for the continent to meet the goal of halving poverty by 2015.

Simultaneously, aspects of the World Trade Organisation (WTO)'s liberal agenda are deeply problematic for Africa's food producers. The Trade-Related Intellectual Property Rights (TRIPS) provisions, which allow for the patenting of food plants, could potentially see African farmers forfeiting the rights to seed variants they have used for generations. Also, given that African farmers are constantly innovating with new strains and methods, they may be robbed of the benefits of their farm-level experiments. African delegations to WTO conferences badly need expertise in negotiating their corner and, fortunately, some enlightened aid partners (including Britain's Department for International Development) have recognised this and provided some assistance.

Making African agriculture pay wouldn't eliminate all famines – it wouldn't stop wars or HIV/AIDS and wouldn't solve the problem of extreme poverty, whereby the poorest simply cannot afford to buy whatever food is available – but it would be a major step in the right direction. It would leave Africa much better placed to reverse its current immiseration.

9 Oxfam, 2002, *Rigged rules and double standards: trade, globalisation and the fight against poverty*, Oxfam www.maketradefair.com, Oxford.

The fiction of charity

Charity food, in large part, is the spin-off of this system of agricultural subsidies. Food aid is a fictitious generosity; the other side of the food-as-global-commodity coin. Food aid also commonly serves as a bribe to those who are already 'eating' in Africa. Food is famously easy to steal (or in aid agency parlance, 'divert') and, even when delivered as intended, it becomes a mechanism for social and political control. The idiom of mercy avoids the necessary politicisation of famine. It panders to the language of charity and beneficence, not rights and entitlements.

The language of charity food and medical aid is profoundly emotive. Typically, it reflects a fairy-tale narrative with innocent 'victims' (African child and her mother) being 'saved' by skilled and benevolent outsiders (aid workers and sometimes the western soldiers who guard them).[10] While food aid can save lives, sometimes on a significant scale, the dominance of this 'story' in the international media has become a persistent misrepresentation. It underplays or ignores both the politics of hunger and the fact that foreign charity is a rather marginal contribution to the survival of those stricken by famine, in comparison to their own efforts. From the African viewpoint, the call to 'feed the world' begs the question, 'who is to do the feeding?'

If the current food shortage in Southern Africa is indeed a structural crisis largely brought about by the AIDS pandemic, then the never-before-seen nightmare of peacetime mass starvation may be emerging as a reality, and tens of millions of Africans may indeed end up as welfare dependants on international benefaction. Every piece of specialist wisdom about African food systems and their underlying resilience and dynamism will be stood on its head. Just as the world's aid donors have at last begun to appreciate that aid is not the answer, and Africa should lead its own development, a cataclysm of immense dimensions means that we must consider reverting to international welfarism on a huge scale.

Alex de Waal is a writer and activist who has worked in Africa for 18 years. He is the author of a number of books including studies of famine and international humanitarianism, and regional peace and security. He is director of Justice Africa.

10 Benthall J, 1993,
*Disasters, relief and the
media*, IB Tauris,
London.

Feast or famine?

Health and environment campaigners should learn the lessons of the anti-tobacco lobby and unite against the food industry.

James Erlichman

The four wings of the food movement must learn to fly in sweeter alignment. If they don't, they risk being swallowed, as single morsels, by the powerful predator they each abhor. Make no mistake – the modern food industry is a predator. Such irony. That which feeds us is (slowly) killing us. The modern food system pretends to nurture when its true aim is merely, most profitably, to feed us – or to pretend that fault lies elsewhere when we slowly starve or bloat into the anguish of obesity.

Let me define my four wings of the food movement: food poverty (in Britain and the developing world); obesity; food hygiene (microbiological and chemical safety); and genetic engineering and irradiation (21st-century manipulation). There is a common cause that many, I believe, fail to see. We have all lost control of our food.

In Britain, over the last 15 years, we have tended to concentrate on the impact of food hygiene and genetic engineering on our lives. This is hardly surprising. First, the *Salmonella* and *Listeria* scandals of the late 1980s hit us. Then we faced the horrible consequences of BSE when transmission to humans was proven, and foot-and-mouth disease added to the escalating unease about the safety of the food chain and the dangers of intensive agriculture. Allied to these deeply felt concerns are the issues of food irradiation and the cloning of Dolly the sheep and subsequent generations of livestock – all done in the unproven belief that we could improve the human food supply simply by applying our brains to better science.

Have food science and technology helped or hurt? Both, of course, but let's look at the evidence. The pounds and pence cost of food has plunged over the past 30 years. That's a narrow fact. Food is cheaper measured by the working hours needed to obtain it. Chicken was a luxury but is now a staple commodity of the cheap fast food industry. This has been 'achieved' by the application of intense breeding, feeding and other scientific techniques to agriculture. Animal welfare and environmental groups have vigorously complained (often in the comparative wilderness) about the true costs, in pain and pollution, of these economic improvements, but these activists have only loosely joined with those primarily concerned that this food science threatens their loved ones. This latter group thinks less about sentient animals and the environment. They worry more – and rightly you may argue – that food science is already bringing increased risk of *Salmonella* and *E.coli* poisoning to today's family dinner table or fast food outlet. Next, there is the nagging fear of incremental pesticide and food additive poisoning their children. Worse still, their adolescents may already be incubating vCJD – the disease caused by BSE that scarily defies all known scientific logic about invading organisms.

Joined-up campaigns

But how much do environmentalists, animal welfarists and sceptics about scientific manipulation of the food supply actually communicate with each other? It seems to me that most spend too much time competing for media attention and public contribution, while failing to find common cause against the powerful food industries that span the globe. They know they and their constituents have lost control of the food supply yet they fail, too often, to work together to regain it. They are, it seems to me, too preoccupied with defending and protecting their own lobby positions at the expense of concerted, effective action. Similarly, those who fight food poverty and malnutrition, on the one hand, and those who fight unhealthy weight gain (obesity) on the other, seldom embrace.

At first glance, of course, food poverty and obesity have nothing in common. Some people have too little food; some, by extreme contrast, have too much. Indeed, the World Watch Institute in Washington recently judged that the dreadful balance is about even: 1.2 billion people in the world have too little to eat while an equal number suffers from unhealthy weight gain. Believing these days that these two groups have nothing in common could not be further from the truth. Traditionally, food poverty campaigners have fought famine, induced largely by nature, or man-made catastrophes of war and civilian destruction. Today, most realise that food poverty is increasingly caused not by food shortages, but by poverty imposed on the poor by economic and political systems which deny them the ability to purchase bounteous local food; the same food that is often exported (in the form of mange-tout and other delicacies) to an all-night supermarket near you. Equally, the obesity epidemic has often been described merely as a disease of opulent and sedentary Westerners – a group too lazy to open the fridge or turn off the TV and devote their attention to creating a nutritious meal, resorting instead to the convenience of the dial-up, take-away pizza.

This modern plague seems to have nothing to do with the food poverty of Africa or the inner cities of the West. In fact, the true cause of both types of malnourishment is loss of control over the food system. The alarming obesity epidemic in affluent Western nations cannot be explained alone by genetic susceptibility among those who eat very little but still gain weight. All of us are fundamentally stuck with the genes of our hunter gatherer ancestors who roamed the Earth for about 4 million years. Those millennia were marked by constant famine and starvation. We were all bred, therefore, to avoid food shortages and to gorge upon and store long-lasting fats and sugars that stood between our ancestors and starvation. Only in the past 50 years (the post-Second World War generations) have we seen this genetic and historical food inheritance flipped upside down. Suddenly, we have too much affordable, attractive, alluring and energy-dense food to eat. Simultaneously, we have been hit by a world of sudden and advanced mechanisation that has destroyed the need to expend energy. We no longer toil in mills or at the mangle. Instead we drive to work to sit at the computer and our kids are seduced by PlayStations and the internet. Of course, some of us will be more prone to weight gain with such sedentary lifestyles than others. But we are all at risk.

The food industry knows just how susceptible we are with our 'famished' hunter gatherer genes coupled with our sedentary 'work' stations. It knows we still cannot resist the famine foods of fat, sugar and salt, which the fast food industry so brilliantly produces in pizzas, burgers, fried chicken and chips. And yet the people who are trying to fight unhealthy weight gain in the West often fail to find common cause with those who fight food poverty abroad. In fact, the two campaigns are joined not only at the hip – but also at the stomach. Pioneering work by David Barker at Southampton University has now proved this link without question.

Barker and his colleagues have demonstrated that food poverty can prove the most pernicious path to obesity. Yes, the most pernicious path to obesity – it is worth repeating. In various epidemiological analyses, Barker has shown that unborn foetuses carried by malnourished mothers learn a metabolic strategy to survive while still in the womb. In other words, the babes adapt to conserve every calorie given to them through their mother to survive womb deprivation, birth trauma and food shortages early in life.

From food poverty to obesity

However, when these children do survive – and their parents move to the mega-cities of the developing world to find work – they become prime candidates for obesity of the most dangerous kind because of their foetal, metabolic re-alignment. Even poor cities today are filled with very cheap fatty foods available on virtually every street corner. Go to Mexico City if you don't believe me. This street food has the attraction that it need not be stored and refrigerated, it requires no cooking or preparation at home, is relatively cheap, accessible and extremely tasty.

The consequence, however, is that even the poorest – those without physically active jobs and education to avoid cheap gluttony – can still afford these fatty and sugary foods which are swallowed into bodies designed by 'womb famine' to preserve every calorie. The result is very sudden and early weight gain leading to abdominal obesity amongst an alarming number of people in urban centres throughout the developing world. The obesity epidemic strikes not only in mid-town Manhattan – it strikes in the meaner streets of Nairobi too. And it also strikes among the poorer populations in every British city. The result is a dramatic increase in heart disease, type two diabetes and other life threatening or limiting conditions among the poorest of our population.

I am not suggesting that all British food campaigners have failed to read between the lines, connect the dots and appreciate the whole picture. On the contrary – the leaders of this largely unsung movement have been exemplary, but unfortunately they have not yet persuaded the media, and therefore the public, that all entries into the food debate are essentially equal and of equal importance. Whether you suspect GM foods, fear pesticides in your children's diets, hate cruelty to animals, campaign to end food poverty abroad or in Britain – or understand just how vital is the battle against the obesity epidemic – then you belong to a common cause.

That common cause is to fight to regain control over the quality and quantity of our food supply. It will be a long struggle. The food industry – be it powerful agricultural landowners, food manufacturers or supermarkets – will be keen to protect its power and its profits. It will not come to the (negotiating) table easily.

The battle against the tobacco industry proves an enlightening model that the food industry has already adopted. The tobacco companies first claimed they were not to blame for lung cancer, heart diseases and other causes of death and disability. Today, the food industry is similarly blaming our sedentary lifestyles for obesity and other diseases and refusing, in the main, to accept its own part in making us overweight, obese and unwell.

And, just like the tobacco industry, it is blaming consumers for their own plight. It tells us we have, and should defend, our powers of choice. That means safeguarding our power to let our children watch junk food advertisements on morning and weekend television if that's what they choose to watch. We should also defend our choice to eat and drink what we want and withstand any criticism from the 'food lentilists' who wish to impose a nanny state that will enable us to stay well enough to enjoy a healthy old age and spend time with our healthy grandchildren. We deserve the choice to kill ourselves. We deserve the choice to be beastly to livestock animals. We deserve the choice to wait to see if we die from vCJD. We deserve the choice to be deformed by GM experiments. We deserve the choice to watch the poor survive starvation only to die from obesity in a single generation. We deserve the choice of gluttony and slow subsequent death ourselves.

I say 'beef bollocks' to this elaborate public relations trickery foisted upon us by the food industry and its loyal armies of scientists, lawyers and public relations merchants. If we can learn better to fly in formation, we can expose and successfully challenge the self-interest of our food industry foe.

James Erlichman writes and broadcasts on food and health policy. He was the consumer affairs and agriculture correspondent of The Guardian, *gave written evidence to the Philips Inquiry on BSE, and is currently exploring scientific food and health policy as a PhD student at the University of Sussex.*

'To them that hath ...': how world trade policies undermine poor producers

In today's world, if you want to avoid hunger, then it's best not to grow food

Barbara Stocking

It is an awful paradox in today's world that if you want to avoid hunger, then it's best not to grow food. Ninety-six per cent of the world's farmers live in developing countries, and agriculture provides the main source of income for themselves and their families – some 2.5 billion people. Despite growing urbanisation, two-thirds of the world's poor still live in rural areas and nearly three-quarters of the workforce of the Least Developed Countries are employed in agriculture. Yet 17 per cent of their populations are already undernourished, even while the demand for food continues to grow.

For most African countries, in particular, agriculture comprises by far the largest proportion of their gross domestic product (GDP). Back in 1970, the daily supply of calories available per head in most African countries was between 2,010 and 2,210. By 1996, however, the daily calory supply per head in some 22 countries south of the Sahara had diminished to 1,580–2,160. Africa's ability to feed itself is in steep decline, exposing its people to mounting risk of hunger.

For various reasons, it could be argued that the countries of Africa represent an extreme case. But they also illustrate a basic truth and they may, worryingly, point the way to a more pessimistic future for the world's poor than is generally considered.

The first part of this truth is that hunger is not caused – or only in certain specific circumstances – by any absolute lack of food. In theory, even today, total food production in most African countries is enough to feed their populations. However, as Professor Amartya Sen and others have shown, hunger is about the failure to gain access to food. Put simply, if you can't grow all your own food then you have to obtain it by other means, which in most cases means buying it. That in turn means you have to have something to sell, which may well also be food of a different type. If the price at which you would normally sell has collapsed and/or the price of food that you want to buy has increased beyond your means to pay for it, then you are in trouble.

The second part is that access to food is therefore about trade. On the one hand, it is about being able to produce enough of something that someone else wants. On the other, it is about someone else producing something you want. In the middle is an exchange, or the market. Poor people lack power in their local markets, which is a major problem. But it is becoming ever more plain that the same applies to their nations. The way the global market works is heavily weighted against poor countries and in favour of the relatively better off. The reason is that, for all the rhetoric about making global trade free and fair, about protecting the poor and encouraging development worldwide, the world's poor have no votes in the US, Europe or other wealthy nations.

Taking from the poor to feed the rich

In the rich north, even in the US, the agricultural sector is a relatively small (and declining) contributor to GDP. In contrast, the agricultural sector in developing countries is critical to everything: food security, poverty reduction and economic growth. It is therefore even more crucial that agricultural trade rules are designed to foster agricultural growth in these countries. However, the system that governs world agricultural trade, the Uruguay Round Agreement on Agriculture (AoA), is inherently unjust. It legalises unfair trading practices by rich countries, thereby denying poorer countries the chance to benefit from their share of the wealth generated by global trade.

The Agreement's main flaw is that it allows rich countries to dump their subsidy-driven surpluses on world markets, depressing prices to levels at which local producers can no longer compete. The consequences are that developing-country domestic markets are undermined, their import dependence increased and export opportunities denied.

To make matters worse – and illustrating the spectacular double standards at play – rich-country members of the World Trade Organisation (WTO), while protecting and subsidising their own producers have, at the same time, been forcing developing countries to open their markets. Haiti, for example, is now one of the most open economies in the world. Under pressure from the IMF and the US, it cut its tariff on rice to a mere 3 per cent. As a result, rice imports – mostly subsidised rice from the US – increased thirty-fold. The price of rice in Haiti has hardly fallen and malnutrition now affects 62 per cent of the population (up from 48% in the early 1980s); only big rice traders and American rice farmers emerge as the winners. In the Philippines too, poverty and malnutrition among the millions of rice and maize farmers have risen steadily since the government deregulated the market.

Dairy dumping is yet another example of the irrationalities of trade policies.[1] Subsidised European milk powder is replacing locally produced milk in Jamaica. Many dairy farmers have had to abandon production because most local processors use cheaper imported milk powder instead. Until the early 1990s, Jamaican farmers were largely protected from these subsidised imports and the sector was doing well. But when the government was forced to liberalise imports as part of World Bank-led adjustment policies, dairy farmers began to suffer. In a further irony, hundreds of thousands of dollars of aid have been spent on supporting the development of Jamaica's dairy farming, while EU export subsidies are undermining the sector.

Subsidy and subsistence

The EU, the World Bank, UN World Food Programme (WFP) and UN Food and Agriculture Organisation (FAO) have all played a critical role in Operation Flood, the world's largest dairy develop-

[1] For detailed analysis, see Black F, 2001, 'Update: dumping in Jamaica: a report on the dairy industry', Novib (Oxfam Netherlands).

ment programme, which has benefited millions of small dairy farmers all over India. They have ploughed more than €2.2bn of financial support into the sector over the last three decades and, last year, India became the world's largest dairy producer, producing 84 million tonnes of milk. The sector includes a network of cooperatives serving more than 10 million farmers in over 80,000 villages. It has become an immensely valuable industry in a country that is home to one-third of the world's poor.

The industry is now seeking to expand into new net dairy-importing markets in south-east Asia, the Gulf, and the southern Mediterranean. However, its efforts are being hampered by unfair competition from subsidised European dairy exports. This year, the FAO cites the EU as offering export subsidies at 60 per cent of the international price for whole milk powder, and 136 per cent of the international price for butter.[2] In a fair trading system, developing countries would have access to measures that give them greater flexibility to protect their smallholder farmers from surges of cheap or unfairly subsidised imports.[3] However, unless the EU stops using more than €1.7bn in annual export subsidies on dairy products, the future of dairy farming in countries such as Jamaica looks bleak indeed.

Not that Europe is the only offender. Last year, cotton farmers in America produced a crop worth US$3bn at world market prices. In return, they received subsidies valued at $4bn – more than the US provides in aid to the whole of Africa. Leaving aside the economics of the lunatic asylum, why does this matter for developing countries? As a major cotton exporter, the US influences world prices, and when its subsidies stimulate overproduction, cotton prices on the world market can slump by around a quarter, depriving other exporters of foreign exchange. As a consequence, cotton exporting countries in sub-Saharan Africa lost an estimated $301 million in export earnings in the 2001–2 season alone. This has disastrous implications for levels of poverty and malnutrition in the cotton exporting countries of the region.

Meanwhile, high tariffs in rich countries continue to limit marketing and diversification opportunities for developing countries. As a result, the liberalisation of agricultural markets has mainly benefited the few transnational companies that dominate agricultural trade, and a tiny minority of wealthy

2 UN FAO, March 2002.
3 For further information, see Oxfam's forth-coming paper on the WTO Agreement on Agriculture, covering analysis of the 'Development Box', November 2002.

landowners in developed countries. Farmers in developing countries captured only 35 per cent of world agricultural exports in 2001 – down from 40 per cent in 1961, as a result of falling commodity prices and high trade barriers.

Fixing the odds

Rich countries have clearly stacked the advantages of the AoA in their own favour. Tailoring the rules to their specific situations, they have secured the right to subsidise their own farmers at almost unlimited levels. Since the introduction of the AoA in 1995, domestic subsidies in the OECD countries have not fallen but actually increased.

Many developing countries that have limited funds to subsidise agricultural development see domestic market protection as the major policy instrument for securing the livelihoods of their rural poor. The AoA, however, has considerably reduced the flexibility they can use to protect their agricultural markets. Future negotiations threaten to reduce that room for manoeuvre even more.

WTO negotiations for a new agricultural agreement are due to be concluded in 2005 but are now reaching a critical phase where the basic rules are being redefined. Instead of working towards rebalancing the current agreement, rich countries are fighting to protect their privileges and completely failing to register the very specific needs of developing countries. Achieving an equitable outcome from the WTO agricultural negotiations will be a litmus test of the so-called Doha Development Round. Developing countries should not sign a new agreement that condones export dumping and prevents the protection of rural livelihoods and food security.

At the same time, as poor countries – and millions of individual poor producers in those countries – find their ability to produce and trade hindered or even ruined by the selfish, greedy and short-sighted trade policies of the rich world, another terrible threat is emerging that casts doubt over future food production predictions.

Across rural Southern Africa young women and men are chronically sick or dying from HIV/AIDS. When sick, they are too weak to cultivate their crops and they must be looked after by relatives, which takes people – usually women – away from their own work in the fields. Older women, too, have to bear the burden of looking after the increasing number of AIDS orphans. In Zambia, where the HIV-infection rate is estimated at 25 per cent, food production in AIDS-affected households is generally 16 per cent lower than the norm. Life expectancy has declined from 52 years in 1980 to an estimated 37 today.

The implications of the HIV/AIDS pandemic are profound. First, African agriculture requires a lot of labour. Without it, production will diminish accordingly. Second, the pandemic has only begun to take hold – relatively speaking – in other parts of the world. In East and South Asia, particularly, HIV rates are beginning to climb alarmingly.

There is now a vicious downward spiral taking hold. Some countries, particularly in Africa, have become highly food insecure, facing a combination of chronic poverty, dependence on low-priced and price-fluctuating exports, high levels of food imports and low levels of domestic supply of essential food crops. These trends, caused partly by unfair global trade rules, will be exacerbated by HIV/AIDS.

A radical change of policies is needed in the rich world. It is time to end all forms of dumping of agricultural products and improve market access conditions for developing countries. It is also time to get serious about HIV/AIDS and mobilise the resources to combat it. Finally, as economist Jeffrey Sachs has argued, in order to meet the 2015 millennium development goals,

> the poorest people in the world are not going to be able to enjoy the benefits of sustainable development without significant, large, continuing net resource transfers from the richest countries. Any idea that this is going to be done in any other way, merely through better governance or through structural adjustment on the part of the poor countries, will not stand up to the evidence.[4]

Barbara Stocking has been director of Oxfam GB since May 2001. Previously, she was a member of the top management team of the NHS. In her eight years with the NHS, she worked as regional director and most recently as director of the Modernisation Agency, charged with modernising the NHS.

4 Quoted in 'Environment matters', *World Bank annual review*, 2002.

Related publications from Demos

Inconvenience Food

Caroline Hitchman, Ian Christie,
Michelle Harrison and Tim Lang
ISBN 1 84180 050 3 £10

That an estimated 4 million people live
in food poverty in an age of abundance
is one of the grim ironies of our age. As
this detailed study shows, it is a form of
social exclusion that is directly linked to
the daily choices many of us make when
buying food. For rational and legitimate reasons, large food retailers target
the 'cash rich, time poor' shopper with
upmarket convenience food, but the low
income shoppers, who are often both
time and cash poor, find themselves
squeezed out of the market. Through
in depth interviews conducted in
people's homes and during shopping
trips, this report provides a compelling
insight into the joyless reality of food
poverty.

System Failure

Jake Chapman
ISBN 1 84180 044 9 £8

The current model of public policy
making is no longer right for a government that has set itself the challenge of
delivering better public services.
Improvements are driven by central
policy initiatives that assume a direct
relationship between action and
outcome. As Jake Chapman explains,
this is a false assumption and government's energetic attempts to force
change from the centre are become
counter-productive. The alternative is

government based on continuous learning, and long-term solutions should rely
more on the inherent adaptability of
complex systems, rather than pushing
for endless efficiency gains through
penalties and incentives.

The Moral Universe

Demos Collection, Issue 16
ISBN 1 84180 024 4 £10

Political conflict is increasingly framed
in ethical terms, within and between
societies. Yet as the dominance of
'western' freedom and progress has
required increased military defence,
western societies are becoming aware of
new challenges to their moral self-confidence. We can barely face the shocking news that our version of the good
society is not universally accepted. In
this collection of essays, a series of
world-leading thinkers illuminate contemporary ethical dilemmas, and artic-
ulate a long-term response to the need
for a 'remoralisation', which can be sus-
tained in a new, more interdependent
world.

The Protest Ethic

John Lloyd
ISBN 1 84180 009 0 £9.95

The radical assurance of the anti-globalisation movement has cast governments, corporations and world trade
bodies in the role of ruthless capitalists
who care little for the world's poor, or
the planet itself. John Lloyd, a

renowned international affairs commentator, argues that by making small, haphazard concessions to these pressure groups, the cause of bringing peace and prosperity to the developing world will actually be hindered. Instead what is needed is fundamental reform of the Bretton Woods institutions, such as the WTO, and true social democracy on a global scale.

Demos publications are available from:

Central Books
99 Wallis Road
London E9 5LN
tel: 020 8986 5488
fax: 020 8533 5821
email: mo@centralbooks.com

Visit our website at www.demos.co.uk for a full list of publications, information on upcoming events and our current reserach programme, and worldwide links.